Stop Faking It!

Finally Understanding Science   So You Can Teach It

LIGHT

Stop Faking It!

Finally Understanding Science   So You Can Teach It

LIGHT

NATIONAL SCIENCE TEACHERS ASSOCIATION

Arlington, Virginia

NATIONAL SCIENCE TEACHERS ASSOCIATION

Claire Reinburg, Director
Andrew Cocke, Associate Editor
Judy Cusick, Associate Editor
Carol Duval, Associate Editor
Betty Smith, Associate Editor

ART AND DESIGN Linda Olliver, Director
   Brain Diskin, Illustrator

NSTA WEB Tim Weber, Webmaster

PERIODICALS PUBLISHING Shelley Carey, Director

PRINTING AND PRODUCTION Catherine Lorrain-Hale, Director
   Nguyet Tran, Assistant Production Manager
   Jack Parker, Desktop Publishing Specialist

PUBLICATIONS OPERATIONS Erin Miller, Manager

sciLINKS Tyson Brown, Manager

NATIONAL SCIENCE TEACHERS ASSOCIATION
Gerald F. Wheeler, Executive Director
David Beacom, Publisher

Light: Stop Faking It! *Finally Understanding Science So You Can Teach It*
   NSTA Stock Number: PB169X3
05   04   4   3   2

Library of Congress Cataloging-in-Publication Data
Robertson, William C.
   Light.
   p. cm. — (Stop faking it!)
   ISBN 0-87355-215-61. Light—Study and teaching (Middle school) 2. Optics—Study
and teaching (Middle school) I. Title.
   QC363.R54 2003
   535'.071'273—dc21
                                                                2003004143

NSTA is committed to publishing quality materials that promote the best in inquiry-based science education. However, conditions of actual use may vary and the safety procedures and practices described in this book are intended to serve only as a guide. Additional precautionary measures may be required. NSTA and the author(s) do not warrant or represent that the procedure and practices in this book meet any safety code or standard or federal, state, or local regulations. NSTA and the author(s) disclaim any liability for personal injury or damage to property arising out of or relating to the use of this book including any recommendations, instructions, or materials contained therein.

SC*i*LINKS.
Featuring sciLINKS®—a new way of connecting text and the Internet. Up-to-the-minute online content, classroom ideas, and other materials are just a click away. Go to page x to learn more about this new educational resource.

Contents

Preface

Back when I was in college, there was a course titled Physics for Poets. At a school where I taught physics, the same kind of course was referred to by the students as Football Physics. The theory behind having courses like these was that poets and/or football players, or basically anyone who wasn't a science geek, needed some kind of watered-down course because most of the people taking the course were—and this was generally true—SCARED TO DEATH OF SCIENCE.

In many years of working in education, I have found that the vast majority of elementary school teachers, parents who home school their kids, and parents who just want to help their kids with science homework fall into this category. Lots of "education experts" tell teachers they can solve this problem by just asking the right questions and having the kids investigate science ideas on their own. These experts say you don't need to understand the science concepts. In other words, they're telling you to fake it! Well, faking it doesn't work when it comes to teaching *anything*, so why should it work with science? Like it or not, you have to understand a subject before you can help kids with it. Ever tried teaching someone a foreign language without knowing the language?

The whole point of the *Stop Faking It!* series of books is to help you understand basic science concepts and to put to rest the myth that you can't understand science because it's too hard. If you haven't tried other ways of learning science concepts, such as looking through a college textbook, or subscribing to *Scientific American*, or reading the incorrect and oversimplified science in an elementary school text, please feel free to do so and then pick up this book. If you find those other methods more enjoyable, then you really are a science geek and you ought to give this book to one of us normal folks. Just a joke, okay?

Just because this book series is intended for the nonscience geek doesn't mean it's watered-down material. Everything in here is accurate, and I'll use math when it's necessary. I will stick to the basics, though. My intent is to provide a clear picture of underlying concepts, without all the detail on units, calculations, and intimidating formulas. You can find that stuff just about anywhere. Also, I'll try to keep it lighthearted. Part of the problem with those textbooks (from elementary school through college) is that most of the authors and the teachers who use them take themselves way too seriously. I can't tell you the number of times I've written a science curriculum only to have colleagues tell me it's "too flip" or "You know, Bill, I just don't think people will get this joke." Actually, I don't really care if you get the jokes either, as long as you manage to learn some science here.

Speaking of learning the science, I have one request as you go through this book. There are two sections titled *Things to do before you read the science stuff* and *The science stuff*. The request is that you actually DO all the "things to do" when I ask you to do them. Trust me, it'll make the science easier to understand, and it's not like I'll be asking you to go out and rent a superconducting particle accelerator. Things around the house should do the trick for most of the activities. This book also includes a few goodies (filters and a diffraction grating) for the activities that require special equipment.

By the way, the book isn't organized this way (activities followed by explanations followed by applications) just because it seemed a fun thing to do. This method for presenting science concepts is based on a considerable amount of research on how people learn best and is known as the *Learning Cycle*. There are actually a number of versions of the Learning Cycle but the main idea behind them all is that we understand concepts best when we can anchor them to our previous experiences. One way to accomplish this is to provide the learner with a set of experiences and then explain relevant concepts in a way that ties the concepts to those experiences. Following that explanation with applications of the concepts helps to solidify the learner's understanding. The Learning Cycle is not the only way to teach and learn science, but it is effective in addition to being consistent with recommendations from *The National Science Education Standards* (National Research Council 1996) on how to use inquiry to teach science. (Check out Chapter 3 of the *Standards* for more on this.) In helping your children or students to understand science, or anything else for that matter, you would do well to use this same technique.

As you go through this book, you'll notice that just about everything is measured in *Système Internationale* (SI) units, such as meters, kilometers, and kilograms. You might be more familiar with the term *metric units*, which is basically the same thing. There's a good reason for this—this is a science book and scientists the world over use SI units for consistency. Of course, in everyday life in the United States, people use what are commonly known as English units (pounds, feet, inches, miles, and the like).

The book you have in your hands, *Light*, covers three different scientific models of what light is. Each model is useful for explaining different kinds of observations. With those three models, you'll be able to understand how and why light bends, how optical instruments form images, what causes rainbows, how to draw 3-D images, and why the sky is blue. There's also an entire chapter on how the eye works. I do not address a number of light topics that you might find in a physical science textbook, choosing instead to provide just enough of the basics so you will be able to figure out those other concepts when you encounter them. You might also notice that this book is not laid out the way these topics might be addressed in a traditional high school or college textbook. That's because this isn't a textbook. You can learn a great deal of science from this book, but it's not a traditional approach.

One more thing to keep in mind: You actually CAN understand science. It's not that hard when you take it slowly and don't try to jam too many abstract ideas down your throat. Jamming things down your throat, by the way, seemed to be the philosophy behind just about every science course I ever took. Here's hoping this series doesn't continue that tradition.

Acknowledgments

The Stop Faking It! series of books is produced by the NSTA Press: Claire Reinburg, director; Carol Duval, project editor; Linda Olliver, art director; Catherine Lorrain-Hale, production director. Linda Olliver designed the cover from an illustration provided by artist Brian Diskin, who also created the inside illustrations.

This book was reviewed by Pamela Gordon (Randall Middle School, Florida); Olaf Jorgenson (Director of Science, Social Sciences, and World Languages, Mesa Public Schools, Arizona); and Daryl Taylor (Williamstown High School, New Jersey).

About the Author

Bill Robertson is a science education writer, teaches online math and physics and trains new faculty for the University of Phoenix, and reviews and edits science materials. His numerous publications cover issues ranging from conceptual understanding in physics to how to bring constructivism into the classroom. Bill has developed K–12 science curricula, teacher materials, and award-winning science kits for Biological Sciences Curriculum Study, the United States Space Foundation, the Wild Goose Company, and River Deep. Bill has a master's degree in physics and a Ph.D. in science education.

How can you avoid searching hundreds of science web sites to locate the best sources of information on a given topic? SciLinks, created and maintained by the National Science Teachers Association (NSTA), has the answer.

In a SciLinked text, such as this one, you'll find a logo and keyword near a concept, a URL (www.scilinks.org), and a keyword code. Simply go to the SciLinks web site, type in the code, and receive an annotated listing of as many as 15 web pages—all of which have gone through an extensive review process conducted by a team of science educators. SciLinks is your best source of pertinent, trustworthy Internet links on subjects from astronomy to zoology.

Need more information? Take a tour—http://www.scilinks.org/tour/

Light—The Early Years

I'm going to start this book with a rather simplistic view of what light is. There are better explanations than the one I'll use in this chapter, and I'll get to those later. We'll start with the simple explanation, though, because it's the easiest to understand and it does explain quite a few things. Also, historically, it's the one that came first; hence, the title of this chapter. Before I get to the explanation, though, you have a few —

Things to do before you read the science stuff

Find yourself a flashlight, a piece of white paper, scissors, cellophane tape, a pen or pencil, an index card, and a mirror with at last one flat edge (a rectangular hand mirror works best). The mirror shouldn't have a frame, so that you can set

1 Chapter

Figure 1.1

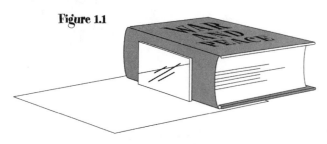

a flat edge directly onto a sheet of paper, as shown in Figure 1.1.

Cut a narrow slit (no more than a few millimeters in width) in the index card, as shown in Figure 1.2.

Now tape the cut index card over the front of the flashlight so the open end of the slit just meets the edge of the flashlight. Check out Figure 1.3.

Figure 1.2

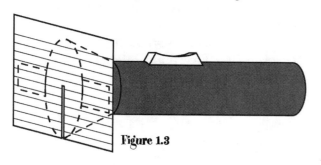

Figure 1.3

Turn on the flashlight and set it on a sheet of white paper that's on a flat surface. Adjust the angle of the flashlight until you get a nar-

row beam of light that is visible all along the paper (Figure 1.4). The beam will probably spread out a bit, but as long as it's not a lot, you'll be okay.

Prop the mirror up against a large, heavy book or other similar object so it's standing vertically on its edge on the sheet of paper. Shine your flashlight beam toward the mirror so you

Figure 1.4

can see both the incoming and the reflected beam on the sheet of paper, as in Figure 1.5.

Now carefully draw an arc that shows the angle the incoming beam makes with the mirror, and another arc that shows the angle the reflected beam makes with the mirror (Figure 1.6).

Figure 1.5

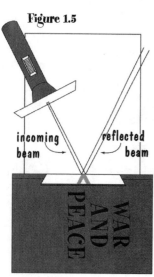

incoming beam → ← reflected beam

WAR AND PEACE

Figure 1.6

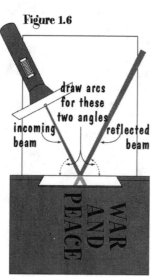

draw arcs for these two angles

incoming beam → ← reflected beam

WAR AND PEACE

2

Repeat this for the beam hitting the mirror at a different angle (Figure 1.7). Then repeat again for a third angle. Once you're done drawing these angles, compare each incoming beam angle with each corresponding reflected beam angle. If you have a protractor (something that measures angles), great. Otherwise, just eyeball it to see whether one is consistently larger or smaller than the other, or whether they're about the same.

The science stuff

Time for that simplistic explanation of light, which is basically that light can be thought of as traveling in *rays,* which move in straight lines until they hit something like a mirror. So, for example, the light emitted from a lightbulb travels outward in a bunch of straight-line rays, as shown in Figure 1.8. To figure out what happens to the light, all you have to do is follow the individual rays that leave the bulb.

What makes this a simplistic explanation of light is the fact that light does not always travel in straight lines.[1] From this point on, I'll refer to this explanation as the *ray model.*[2]

Let's use the ray model of light to describe what happens when light reflects off a mirror. We can represent the incoming and reflected beams of light each as a single ray of light. Actually, the beams

Figure 1.7

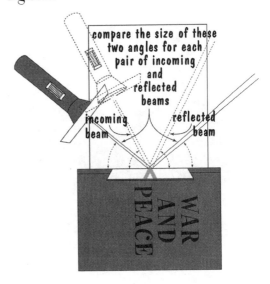

compare the size of these two angles for each pair of incoming and reflected beams

incoming beam

reflected beam

WAR AND PEACE

Figure 1.8

Light from a lightbulb travels outward in the form of rays that move in straight lines

---

[1] Many elementary school textbooks state, incorrectly, that light always travels in straight lines. We'll see later that this just isn't true. By the time you finish this book, maybe you'll do like I do and cringe every time you read that mistake in a textbook.

---

[2] The term *ray model* refers to the fact that representing light as rays is a scientific model. More on what a scientific model is later in this chapter.

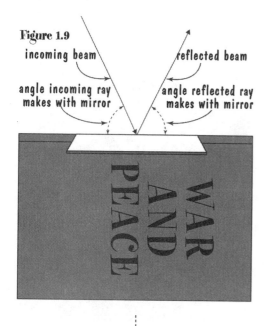

Figure 1.9

incoming beam

reflected beam

angle incoming ray
makes with mirror

angle reflected ray
makes with mirror

WAR
AND
PEACE

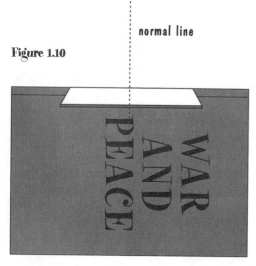

Figure 1.10

normal line

WAR
AND
PEACE

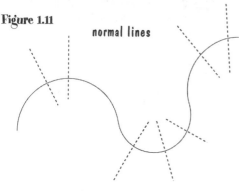

Figure 1.11

normal lines

consist of a large number of rays of light, but we're just focusing on one ray per beam. Then the mirror situation looks like Figure 1.9.

If you drew and measured carefully, you undoubtedly discovered that the angle the incoming beam (or ray) makes with the mirror is equal to the angle the reflected beam (or ray) makes with the mirror. Actually, you probably *didn't* get exactly the same angle measures because a) your light beam spread out a bit, making it difficult to get an exact angle, and b) you didn't draw and measure all that carefully because you're not getting a grade on this project, thank you very much. If you didn't get exactly equal angles, trust me—with a very narrow beam of light and careful measurement, you'll get exactly equal angles every time.

So now you know how reflected light behaves, except for the fact that I had you measure the wrong angles! Well, not exactly the *wrong* angles, but not the angles scientists use when describing reflection of light. In order to use the scientifically correct angles, I have to define something known as the *normal* to a surface. A line that is *normal* to a surface is one that is perpendicular to that surface. Figure 1.10 shows the normal line for our mirror.

For a curved surface, the normal to the surface is in a different direction at each part of the surface, as shown in Figure 1.11.

At any rate, the angles we should measure if we're good little scientists are the angles the incoming and reflected beams make with the line that is normal to the reflecting surface. When we use those angles, they're called the *angle of incidence* and the *angle of reflection,* respectively.

Turns out these two angles are also equal to each other for any reflected beam of light (Figure 1.12). Don't believe me? Measure them.

With the properly defined angles, we can now write down what's known as the **law of reflection,** which is that:

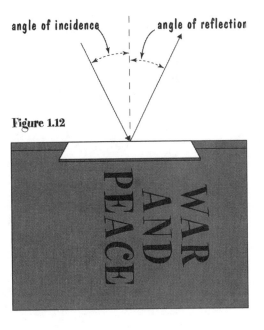

Figure 1.12

Angle of incidence = angle of reflection

Okay, big deal. If you've ever looked at a book about light, you've seen the law of reflection written down somewhere, so why did we just spend a whole lot of time getting to it? There are a couple of reasons. First, it's important that you actually experience something before I formalize it. If you did what I asked, then you saw firsthand that the angle of incidence is equal to the angle of reflection. That experience beats the heck out of believing something just because it's written down in a book. Second, I took the time to explain that picturing light as a bunch of rays that travel in a straight line is just one model of what light is. The ray model is useful for explaining reflection of light but not so useful for explaining other things that light does. One of the keys to understanding science is understanding what a scientific model is and understanding the limitations of whatever model you're using. In that vein, keep the following in mind.

People who develop science concepts *make them up.* These ideas are *not* handed down from deities on high and they are not facts. What makes concepts and models hang around is that they help explain and predict observations. If they cease to do that, they gradually go to the scientific model graveyard. That said, it's not as if you can come up with any old explanation and call it a valid scientific theory. There are conventions for evaluating theories to determine how good they are. The theories, or models, that are in this book have been around awhile, so you can be pretty sure they won't be out of vogue tomorrow.

Before moving on, let's recap. I introduced a ray model of light and used it to explain how reflected light behaves. I introduced *normal lines* and the fact that scientists measure the angles that light rays make with the normal line, rather than the angles the light makes with the reflecting surface.

SCI*L*INKS.
THE WORLD'S A CLICK AWAY

Topic: reflection

Go to: *www.scilinks.org*

Code: SFL01

More things to do before you read more science stuff

In this section, you're going to see what happens when light travels from one substance to another. In the explanation section that follows, I'll use a ray model of light to explain what's going on.

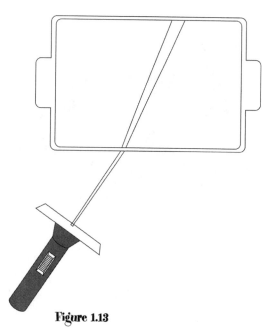

Figure 1.13

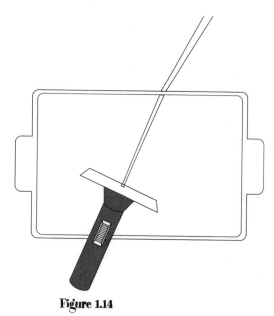

Figure 1.14

If you happen to have a solid, rectangular block of glass, Lucite, or other thick, transparent material, get it. If you don't have anything like that, and I expect that's the case, find a rectangular clear glass or Pyrex baking pan and fill it with water. I'll assume from here on that you're using the pan of water, but everything applies to the other props. Also, grab the flashlight and index card thingie you put together in the first part of this chapter.

Place the pan of water on a flat surface and dim the lights in the room or turn them off altogether. Shine your narrow beam of light towards the pan of water so you can see the beam on the flat surface before it hits the side of the pan (Figure 1.13).

You should be able to see what happens to the light beam after it crosses into the water. If not, move the flashlight around a bit until you can. [Hint: The direction the beam is moving should change once it hits the water.]

If the light gods are smiling upon you, you will be able to trace the path of the light beam all the way through the water, and then when it emerges from the other side of the pan. More likely, though, the light beam sort of dies out after it's in the water. If that's the case, shine your flashlight from above the pan so you can see what the light beam does when traveling from the water back into air (Figure 1.14). [Hint: The beam should change direction again as it travels from the water to the air.]

More science stuff

If you were able to follow the light beam as it went from air to water and then back out into the air, you should have seen something like Figure 1.15.

Figure 1.15

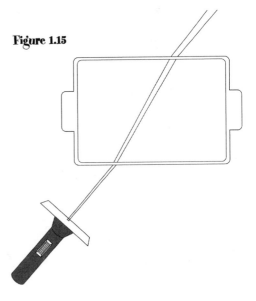

This means that light rays bend, or change direction, when they travel from air to water and from water to air. Of course, this doesn't just happen with air and water. Whenever light travels from one substance to another, it bends. This bending is known as **refraction.** And just so we have the correct terminology, scientists talk about light traveling from one **medium**[3] to another, rather than from one substance to another. Water and air are different mediums, sugar water and plain water are different mediums, cold water and hot water are different mediums, and Miss Cleo and John Edward are different mediums.

It's natural to ask *why* light refracts in traveling from one medium to another. In fact, that "why" question is what causes scientists to develop scientific models. Later on, I'll introduce a scientific model of light that provides a pretty good explanation of refraction. Our current ray model, however, doesn't do much to help us understand the reason for refraction.[4]

Figure 1.16

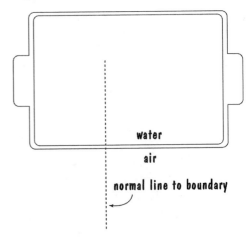

water

air

normal line to boundary

The ray model does help *describe* what's going on with refraction, though. For that description, we can use our old friend the *normal* to a surface. Figure 1.16 shows a top view of the boundary between air and water, with the normal to that boundary drawn in.

---

[3] See the second or third definition of this word in your local dictionary.

---

[4] Actually, there's something known as Fermat's principle that, when coupled with a ray model, provides an explanation of refraction. Because it's kind of a strange principle, I'll address it in the Applications section rather than get totally off track here.

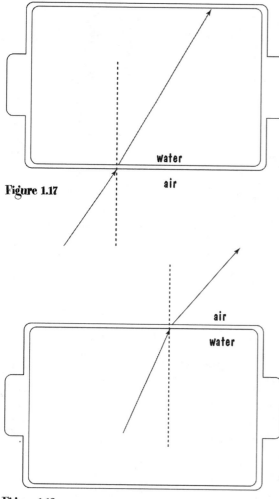

Figure 1.17

Figure 1.18

When a light ray travels from air to water, it refracts as shown in Figure 1.17. When a light ray travels from water to air, it refracts as shown in Figure 1.18.

Now, water is more *dense* than air,[5] so we might be tempted to generalize our result and say the following:

> When light travels from a less dense medium to a more dense medium, it refracts *towards* the normal. When light travels from a more dense medium to a less dense medium, it refracts *away from* the normal.

And by golly, that turns out to be true in all cases. In fact, there's a mathematical relationship that describes exactly how much and in what direction light bends when it goes from one medium to another. If I could be sure everyone had a nice, uniform block of Lucite, I could have you sort of "discover" that relationship for yourself, just as I had you "discover" the law of reflection. But since most of you are dealing with a crude baking pan filled with water, I'm just going to give you the relationship. Before I do that, though, I have to define something known as the **index of refraction.** It's represented by the letter *n*, and each medium has its own value of *n*. Basically, the denser the medium, the higher the index of refraction of that medium.[6] The index of refraction of a vacuum (meaning *empty space* rather than something Mr. Oreck

---

[5] The more dense a medium is, the more "stuff" it has in a given volume. This usually means that its molecules are more closely packed together than in a less dense medium.

---

[6] The exact definition of the index of refraction of a medium is the speed of light in that medium divided by the speed of light in a vacuum (empty space). We'll discuss in Chapter 2 why the speed of light should have something to do with the value of *n*.

would like you to buy) is 1.0, the index of refraction of water is 1.33, and the index of refraction of glass is about 1.5.

Okay, so now it's time to write that relationship. You won't immediately recognize everything, so don't freak out, all right?

$$n_1\sin\theta_1 = n_2\sin\theta_2$$

Note for the math phobic

Just so you don't get totally intimidated by the symbols in an equation, here's a brief explanation. An equals sign means that whatever is on the left side of the sign is numerically the same as what's on the right hand side. If two things are in parentheses and next to each other, as in (speed)(time), that means you multiply the two together. If there's a slash between those parentheses, as in (distance)/(time), you divide the first by the second. If there are just letters and no parentheses, two letters next to each other, as in vt, should be multiplied and two letters with a slash in between, as in d/t, means divide the first by the second.

Figure 1.19 will be a big help in understanding this relationship.

We have light going from medium 1 to medium 2, which can be, for example, light going from air into glass. The index of refraction of medium 1 is n_1 and the index of refraction of medium 2 is n_2. θ is the Greek letter "theta." θ_1 is the *angle* between the incident light ray and the normal line, and θ_2 is the angle between the refracted light ray and the normal line. Now sin θ means you take the sine of the angle θ. What's a sine? Well, think back to high school math and things called sines and cosines. If you want to look up the actual definition of sines and cosines, feel free to do that. Suffice it to say they have to do

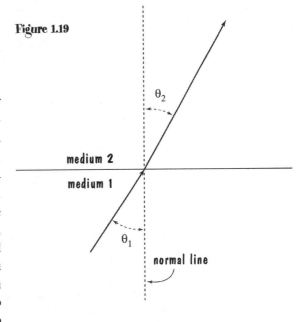

Figure 1.19

with how a particular angle relates to the triangle it might be part of. You don't really need the formal definitions, though, because we aren't going to be calculating any numbers with our relationship. Oh, and by the way, $n_1\sin\theta_1 = n_2\sin\theta_2$ is known as **Snell's law.**

Snell's law works for all different mediums and it has built into it the whole business of refracting toward or away from the normal. I'll do one example to convince you of that. Suppose you shine a light beam from air into a sold block of glass and you do it at a 30-degree angle to the normal (Check out Figure 1.20). We already know what's going to happen—the light will bend towards the normal because it's going from a less dense to a more dense medium.

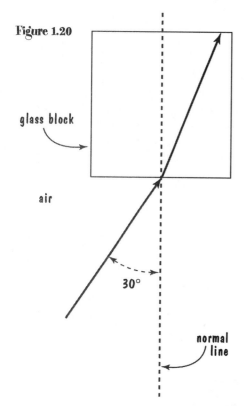

Figure 1.20

glass block

air

30°

normal line

Snell's law will tell us exactly how much the light refracts towards the normal. The index of refraction of air is almost equal to 1, so we'll just let it be 1, and the index of refraction of glass is about 1.5. Snell's law gives us:

$$n_1 \sin\theta_1 = n_2 \sin\theta_2$$

or, in this particular case:

$$n_{air} \sin\theta_{air} = n_{glass} \sin\theta_{glass}$$

Putting in the values for the n's and θ's, we get:

$$(1.0)(\sin 30°) = (1.5)(\sin\theta_{glass})$$

It helps here if you remember that sets of parentheses next to each other mean multiplication. I'm not going to bother you with the algebra we have to do to solve for θ_{glass} (you're welcome)[7], so you can just trust me that the result is:

$$\theta_{glass} = 17.5°$$

This angle is smaller than 30°, meaning the light beam refracts towards the normal. Okay, neat. We can describe exactly what light will do when going from one medium to the next, but keep in mind that it is just a description. Snell's law doesn't do anything to explain *why* light refracts.

Time for another recap. I used a ray model of light to describe exactly how light behaves when traveling from one medium to another. That exact description is Snell's Law, which is a bit more complicated than the law of reflection I introduced earlier.

SCILINKS®

THE WORLD'S A CLICK AWAY

Topic: refraction

Go to: *www.scilinks.org*

Code: SFL02

---

[7] For those of you who really want to see the steps, here's how it goes. First divide both sides of the equation by 1.5. After doing the math on the left side, you get 0.33 = $\sin\theta_{glass}$. This means that $\sin\theta_{glass}$ is equal to 0.33. The angle whose sine is 0.33 is 17.5°, which you can figure out on your calculator or look up in a table of sines.

Even more things to do before you read even more science stuff

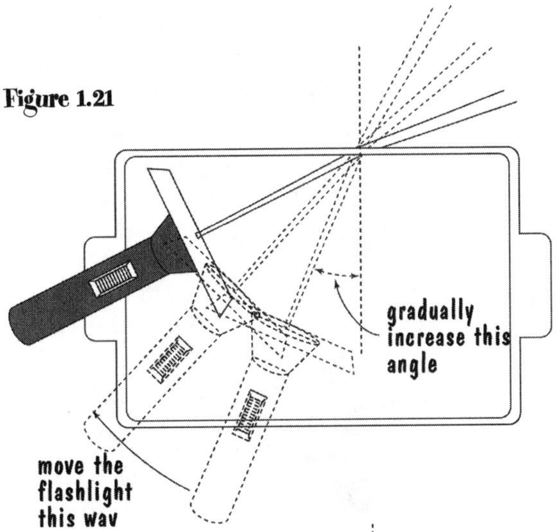

Set up your light beam and pan of water as in Figure 1.14, so the light travels from the water out into the air. The beam should refract away from the normal, yes? Now gradually increase the angle between the incoming beam and the normal, as in Figure 1.21.

Keep doing this until the refracted beam is almost parallel with the edge of the pan. Keep increasing the angle beyond this point, and you will get to where the entire light beam is reflected back into the water as in Figure 1.22.

Figure 1.21

gradually increase this angle

move the flashlight this way

Figure 1.22

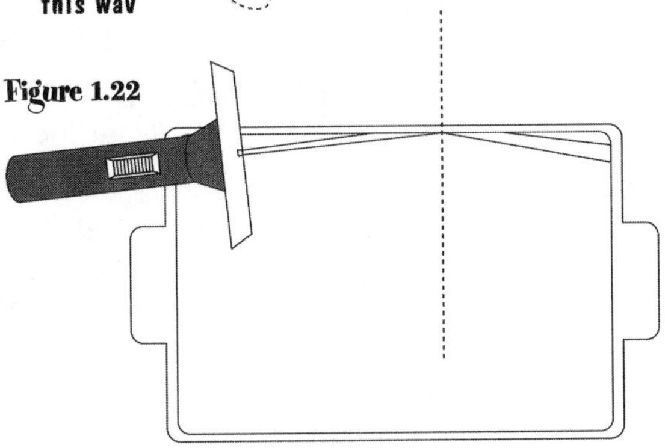

Even more science stuff

What you just observed is known as **total internal reflection.** If you were really observant in earlier sections, you might have noticed that even when the light beam travels on into the second medium, some of the beam is always reflected. The greater the angle between the incident beam and the normal, the more light is reflected rather than refracted. (You might want to go back to your setup and verify this. Then again, maybe not!) Beginning at a certain angle, known as the **critical angle,** *all* of the light is reflected.

And this is how fiber optics works. When you send light into the end of a tube made of Lucite or glass or other dense, transparent substance, the light keeps traveling along the tube, undergoing total internal reflection each time it hits the side (Figure 1.23).

light in   light out

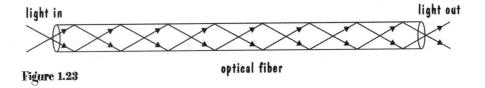

Figure 1.23   optical fiber

So now you know how those cool lights you get at gift shops work. You know, the ones that have dozens of thin, glass-like strands that fan out in a circle from the center, but only light up at the tips, as in Figure 1.24. All the light starts at the base of the lamp, and undergoes total internal reflection all the way out to the tips. If one of the strands bends in the middle, the middle lights up because you've created a spot where the light hits the side at something less than the critical angle, and it escapes.

Figure 1.24

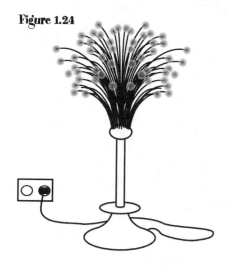

We also use fiber optic cables to send information from one place to another. We just have to turn the entering light on and off really fast. The rate at which the light turns off and on can carry information. It's sort of like sending Morse code by turning a flashlight on and off. Of course, the on and off of a fiber optic cable is about a gazillion times faster than turning a flashlight on and off.

If you're in the mood for a field trip, head to your local rock shop and ask to see a piece of *ulexite*. Place the ulexite over some newsprint for a neat effect. It turns out ulexite is made of tiny strands that act just like optical fibers, so you can read the print at the top surface of the ulexite, demonstrated in Figure 1.25.

And even more things to do before you read even more science stuff

Now that you know something about reflection and refraction, it's time to get to something a bit more interesting. In this section, we'll focus on the images we see as a result of various reflections and refractions.

Find yourself any old mirror—the bathroom mirror will work. Hold up an ob-

Figure 1.25

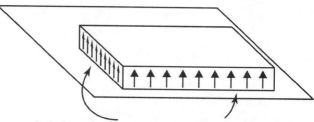

light from the picture travels up to the surface of the ulexite, just as light travels along an optical fiber

ject and look at its reflection in the mirror. How far does the reflected object appear to be from you?

Take a stab at using a diagram of light rays to explain why the object appears where it is and how far away it is.

Look at your reflection in the back of a metal spoon. See if you can explain why your face looks the way it does. Is this an improvement in your facial features?

Figure 1.26

Person holds this object while looking at its reflection in the mirror

Get a glass of water and stick your finger inside. Look at your finger from the side and notice how the image of your finger changes as you move your finger around the glass. See if you can explain what's going on.

And even more science stuff

To figure out why you see what you see when looking at various reflected and refracted images of an object, it helps to imagine that the object is emitting light rays that travel outward in all directions.[8] By tracing the paths of just a few of these rays, we can figure out what's going on. Let's start with the simple one—looking at the reflection of an object in a mirror (Figure 1.26). I'm going to draw a light ray that goes from the object, reflects off the mirror, and goes to your eye.

Now forget the fact that you know this light is reflected off a mirror. If you didn't know you were looking at reflected light, where would you say this light ray originated? In other words, where does the actual object appear to be? Well, the light ray has traveled a total distance of $2d$ (see Figure 1.27), so we think the object is a distance $2d$ away from us.[9] Being ignorant and not knowing this is a reflection, we also assume the light rays that leave the object travel in straight lines and don't bounce off things, so we think the ob-

Figure 1.27

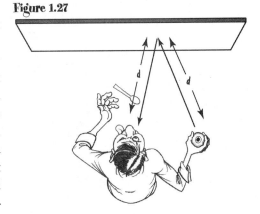

---

[8] Unless the object creates its own light, the light it emits is actually reflected light.

---

[9] We use all sorts of cues to judge distance, such as the size of the image and the difference between what the left eye and right eye see.

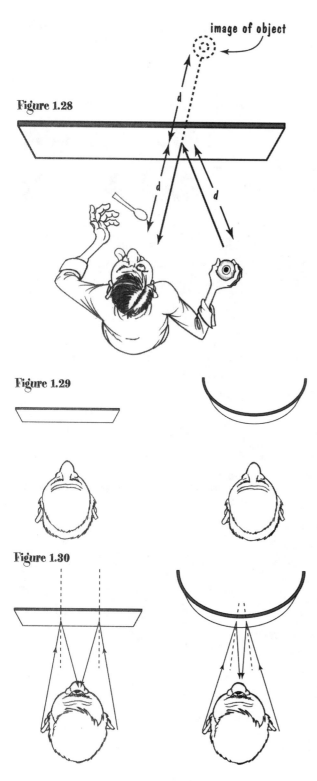

Figure 1.28

Figure 1.29

Figure 1.30

ject is a straight-line distance of 2*d* away from us. In other words, we see the image of the object *behind* the mirror (Figure 1.28).

This is true of all images you see in a flat mirror. They're behind the mirror, and they're just as far behind the mirror as the actual object is in front of the mirror.

All right, what about curved mirrors, and in particular, the back of a spoon? Let's trace the light rays you see when looking at your own reflection in the spoon. Figure 1.29 shows a top view of your head and a flat mirror, and a top view of your head and a curved mirror (the spoon).

For convenience, let's assume you're a cyclops with only one eye in the middle of your head (apologies to all the cyclopses out there). I'm going to draw light rays that leave your ears, reflect off the mirror (flat or curved), and travel to your eye. Those rays are shown in Figure 1.30.

Notice that, for each reflection, the angle of incidence equals the angle of reflection, and those angles are the ones made with the normal line at each reflection point. Also notice that the direction of the normal line changes quite a bit across the surface of the curved mirror. If you're really careful in drawing those lines, you get the result in Figure 1.30. To see what your reflection looks like, just figure out where whose rays that hit your eye *appear* to come from, assuming they travel in a straight line instead of reflecting. I've done that in Figure 1.31.

As you can see, your reflection in a flat mirror is the same size as your actual head. In the curved mirror, though, your head appears to be shrunken in width. The more sharply curved the mirror is, the more shrunken your head appears to be. See Figure 1.32.

Take a close look at the spoon, and you'll see that it is curved more sharply from side to side than it is along its length. See Figure 1.33.

Therefore, the image of your head shrinks more along one direction than along the other, making your head look long and skinny, or short and wide, depending on how you hold the spoon.

Okay, on to how your finger looks in a glass of water. When you have it on the far side of the glass, away from your eyes, it looks pretty darned fat. To see why, what say we draw, umm—light rays! Instead of being reflected, the light rays you see have been *refracted* as they travel from your finger, through the water, and out into the air to your

Figure 1.31

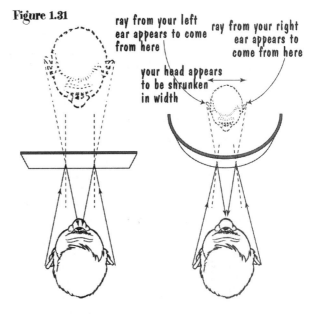

ray from your left ear appears to come from here

ray from your right ear appears to come from here

your head appears to be shrunken in width

Figure 1.32

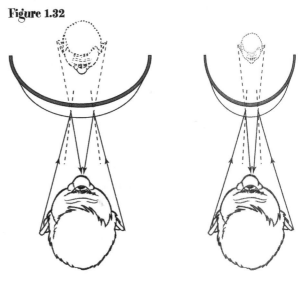

Figure 1.33

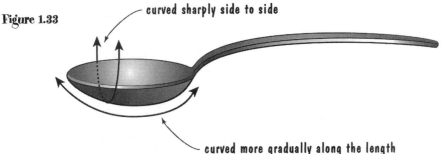

curved sharply side to side

curved more gradually along the length

eyes.[10] Again, I'll assume you are a cyclops and I'll just draw the rays that go from the edges of your finger. In going from a more dense medium (water) to a less dense medium (air), the rays will bend *away from the normal*, and since the side of the glass is curved, the normal will be in a different direction at different parts of the glass. The diagram of light rays is in Figure 1.34. Note that the figure shows only two selected light rays—those that leave the sides of your finger and eventually, after refracting, reach your eye. When those rays leave your finger, they are not initially headed for your eye. After they refract, however, they go towards your eye. Any light rays that start out headed for your eye won't reach it, because they'll refract when they get to the glass-air interface.

As with reflection, your uninformed eye doesn't know the light has been refracted. Your eye assumes the light rays hitting it traveled in a straight line. To figure out the image your eye sees, we trace the rays that hit it back along the direction they came from, as in Figure 1.35.

Your eye sees the image of your finger that's dotted in Figure 1.35. In other words, your finger looks much larger to you than it really is.[11] When your finger is on the side of the glass closest to you, the effect isn't nearly as pronounced. Figure 1.36 shows why.

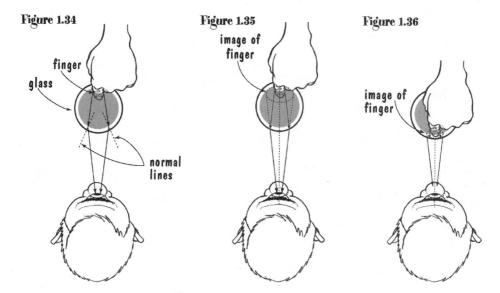

Figure 1.34

finger
glass
normal lines

Figure 1.35

image of finger

Figure 1.36

image of finger

---

[10] You might notice that I'm ignoring the glass that holds the water. To be completely accurate, I should include the refraction that happens when going from water to glass and then from glass to air. All that would do is make our diagrams more complicated, and who needs that? The basic idea is still the same.

---

[11] A little foreshadowing here. Can you think of a use for something that makes objects look bigger than they actually are? Sure you can.

Chapter Summary

- One model for light is that it is composed of rays that travel out in all directions from a light source.

- When light rays go from one medium to another, the light rays could be a) totally reflected back into the original medium, b) partially reflected and partially transmitted into the second medium, or c) totally transmitted into the second medium.

- Reflected light obeys the law of reflection, which states that the angle of incidence is equal to the angle of reflection. Those angles are the angles between the incident and reflected rays and the *normal* to the reflecting surface.

- When light travels from one medium to another, it often bends, or *refracts*. Snell's law describes the exact relationship between the incident and refracted rays.

- The *index of refraction* of a substance is a measure of how dense the substance is and also a measure of how much light refracts when it travels from one medium to another.

- When light travels from a more dense to a less dense medium, there is a chance that the incoming light gets *totally internally reflected*, meaning it reflects back into the more dense medium. This phenomenon is the basis for fiber optics.

- To figure out where a reflected or refracted image is formed, you first draw light rays that come from the original object. Then you trace these rays back along the line of the rays that come straight to the viewer. Where the rays *appear* to come from is where the image is.

Applications

1. When you walk by a store or restaurant window, you not only can see the inside of the store or restaurant, you can see a reflection of yourself. Why is that? Well, remember that, unless you're dealing with total internal reflection, when light travels from one medium to another, some of the light refracts and travels on into the second medium, and some of the light reflects. So, the light coming off you hits the window. Some travels on through, so the people inside can see you and talk about you. Some is also reflected, so you can check out just how much the wind has messed with your hair. Of course, the same thing happens in reverse, so you can see the people inside and they can see a reflection of themselves (see Figure 1.37, next page).

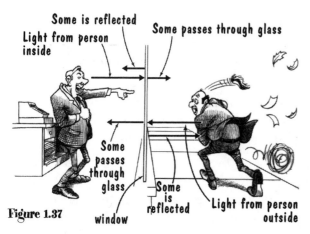

Figure 1.37

Two-way mirrors work the same way. These mirrors are silvered, but not so much that some of the light from you doesn't travel on through so someone behind the mirror can see you. And that's the main point of two-way mirrors; someone uses them to spy on someone else, as shown in Figure 1.38.

But wait a minute. If the mirror isn't completely silvered, shouldn't the person in front of the mirror be able to see light coming from the person behind the mirror? Yes, that would be true *if* there were any lights on in the room behind the mirror. But the people doing the observing keep that room dark, so nothing in it, including the person be-

Figure 1.38

hind the mirror spying on you, emits any significant light for you to see.

Because it's related, I now have to tell you how they make ghosts in the Haunted House at Disneyland. As you ride along in your chair, you see an empty room in front of you. You also see ghosts moving around. Those ghosts are just images that are reflected from a transparent screen in front of you. The real objects (the ones that lead to the ghost images) are actually below you. Check out Figure 1.39.

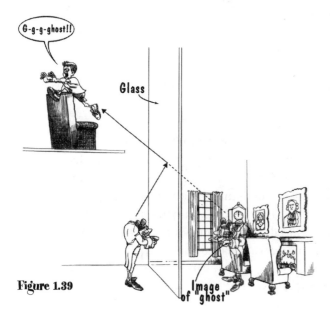

Figure 1.39

2. I remember as a kid riding in the car on a long stretch of road in the Arizona desert, seeing what looked like water on the road up ahead. Of course this had to be a mirage, because as everyone knows, it rains only two thousandths of an inch a year in Arizona. Okay, not true. Anyway, what causes these mirages? Well, on very hot summer days, you often get a temperature inversion, in which the air near the road is much hotter than the air above it, and the change from hotter to cooler air is gradual. The hotter air is less dense than the cooler air.[12] The result is that light from the sky refracts as it travels from the more dense air to the less dense air, and gives you the situation shown in Figure 1.40.

When you trace the light rays reaching your eyes back along the direction from which they came, you see that there's an image of the sky smack dab in the middle of the road up ahead (Figure 1.41). Sure looks like water! Of course, the refracting light ray shown isn't the only one emitted by that patch of sky. That patch of sky also emits light rays that travel straight to you, so you still see the sky where it's supposed to be.

Figure 1.40

Sky

Actual path that light from the sky takes

Figure 1.41

sky

image of sky

Where the light from the sky appears to be coming from

---

[12] See the *Stop Faking It!* book *Energy* for an explanation of this.

Figure 1.42

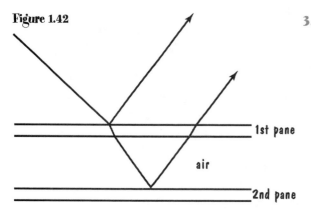

1st pane

air

2nd pane

3. In our house we have a security system with little red and green lights. I still get a little freaked out when I see the reflection of these lights in a window, because there are two sets of lights in the reflection, giving more of an impression of a tiny alien spaceship than a set of security lights. The reason I see two sets of lights is that the windows are double-pane windows. Figure 1.42 shows what happens to the red and green lights.

When the light from a security light hits the inside pane, some is reflected and some refracts on through. The refracted light emerges from the other side of the window pane, passes through the air space between the panes, and reflects off the second pane. Some of the light travels back through the second pane, and the result is that you end up with two images of each light. Either that or it's a tiny alien spaceship.

4. Here's sort of a homework problem. First, look in a regular, flat mirror. Right and left are reversed, right? Use the diagram in Figure 1.43 to figure out why.

Now see if you can set up two flat mirrors so they're at right angles. Look at yourself in this setup. Now right and left are no longer reversed. Use the ray diagram in Figure 1.44 to figure out why.

Figure 1.43

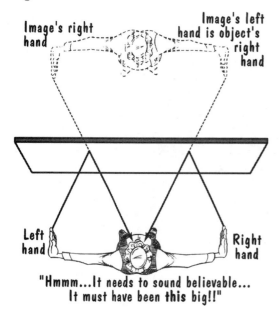

Image's right hand

Image's left hand is object's right hand

Left hand

Right hand

"Hmmm...It needs to sound believable... It must have been this big!!"

Figure 1.44

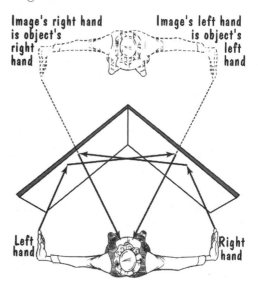

Image's right hand is object's right hand

Image's left hand is object's left hand

Left hand

Right hand

5. I promised in one of the footnotes that I'd explain Fermat's principle. It's kind of esoteric, so if you want to skip this, no big deal. It won't affect your understanding of the rest of the book.

Anyway, here are a few questions. How does light "know" that it has to obey the law of reflection? Instead of the angle of incidence being equal to the angle of reflection, why can't you have something like Figure 1.45?

Figure 1.45

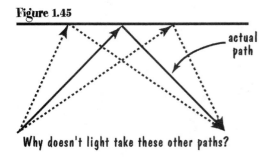

Why doesn't light take these other paths?

Figure 1.46

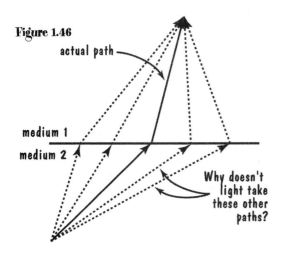

Also, how does light "know" that it has to obey Snell's law? Shown in Figure 1.46 is the path light takes when it obeys Snell's law (let's suppose I calculated it and drew it exactly). But why can't the light travel in the other paths shown?

Well, a French nobleman and mathematician named Pierre de Fermat came up with—surprise—Fermat's principle. The principle states that when light goes from one place to another, it travels a path that takes equal or less time than any nearby paths.[13] It turns out that the paths that obey the law of reflection and Snell's law also obey Fermat's principle.

Fine, but how does the light know to take the least amount of time? Here's where it gets a little strange. The path of least time actually is the *most probable* path for the light to take. The nearby paths are so much less likely to occur, that we never see light take them. Now here's where it gets even weirder. If you go beyond Fermat's time to the 1900s, you can explain what happens by saying that light actually *does* take those nearby paths, but the effect of taking them cancels out. It's still based on probability, but it's as if the light tests out all the nearby paths and figures out that the least-time path is the proper result. Of course, light doesn't have a mind of its own—I don't think.

Topic: properties of light

Go to: *www.scilinks.org*

Code: SFL03

---

[13] Note that the path of least time isn't necessarily the shortest path. That's because light travels at different speeds in different mediums (see Chapter 2), meaning it might be quicker to have most of the path traveled in the faster medium, even if the overall path in both mediums is longer.

Colorful Waves

I know you're probably really upset that all you have so far is a simple little ray model of light. When do we get to the good stuff, you say? How about now? As a bonus, you get to look at lots of pretty colors.

Things to do before you read the science stuff

Figure 2.1

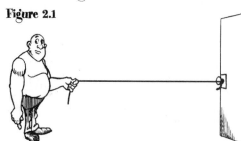

Figure 2.2

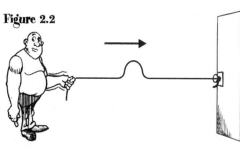

Figure 2.3

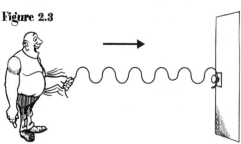

Grab yourself a thin rope or a long section (maybe 10 meters) of latex tubing (try a medical supply store). Tie one end of the rope or tubing to a doorknob or some other fixed object (Figure 2.1).

Quickly move the free end up and down once. You should see a wave pulse move down the rope (I'll assume from here on that you're using a rope), as shown in Figure 2.2.

Now move the rope up and down several times in rapid succession to see if you can get several pulses on the rope at once, as shown in Figure 2.3.

This is a little difficult to see because you have reflected pulses heading back from the other end. Even though those reflected pulses cause trouble, try to see a difference when you make several pulses quickly and when you make them even more quickly (or as scientists say, "really fast"). Look for any difference in the distance between individual pulses.

Now get a large, shallow pan of water. This should be at least the size of pie pan, but even larger is better. In fact, if you have a pond or lake nearby, that would be the best place to do this. Poke the tip of your finger in the center of the pan. You should see ripples traveling outward from your finger, much like ripples in a pond when you drop a rock in it. Dexterity time. Repeatedly poke your finger in the center of the pan. First do it at a relatively slow rate, say two pokes a second. Then do it as fast as you can. Notice any difference in the ripples when you change from slow to fast? Go back and forth between the two rates until you see a clear difference.

The science stuff

Since I had you make a bunch of waves in the previous section, you might jump to conclusions and think I'm going to tell you we can model light as a bunch of waves. That would be correct, so let's learn a little bit about waves.

Figure 2.4

causes wave that moves to the side

up and down motion

up and down motion

Figure 2.5

faster up and down motion

waves are smaller and closer together

First, you might have noticed that an up-and-down motion on your part, both for the rope and the water, produced waves that traveled to the side (Figure 2.4).

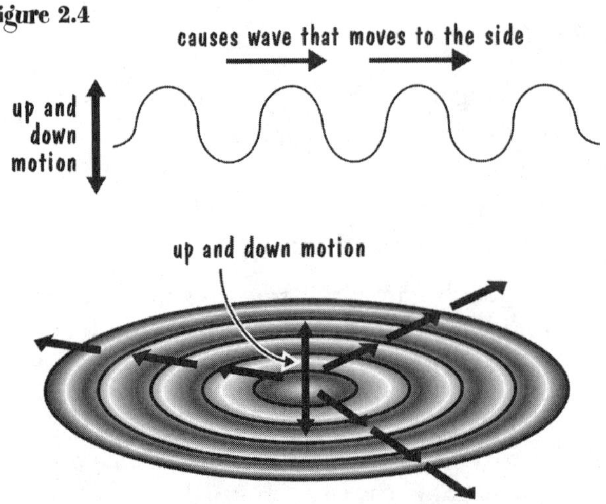

To be more precise, the waves traveled *perpendicular to* the direction of motion of whatever caused them. Waves like this are known as **transverse waves.**

The second thing you might have noticed is that the faster you move up and down to create the waves, the closer together they are (Figure 2.5). In other words, the waves themselves are smaller. If you didn't notice that, go back and do it again. I'll wait.

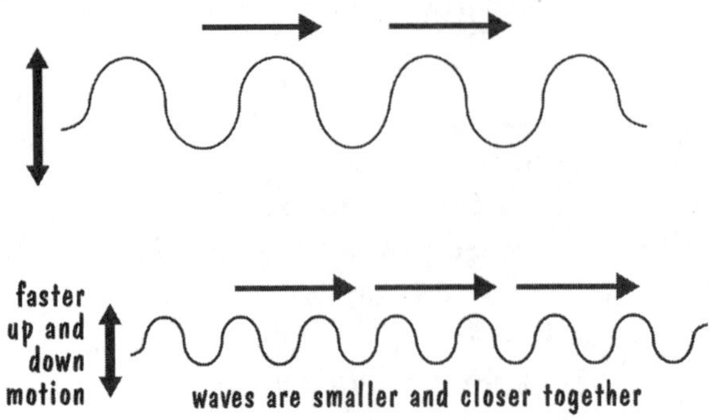

With smaller waves that are closer together, more of them pass a given point in a given time than do larger and farther apart waves. In order to keep track of the size of waves and how fast they pass a given point, we have a couple of definitions.

wavelength. The distance in which a series of waves repeats itself.[1] A couple of examples are shown in Figure 2.6.

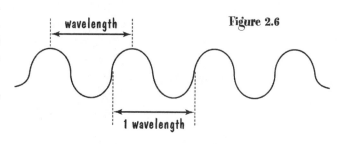

Figure 2.6

wavelength

1 wavelength

frequency. The number of wavelengths that pass a given point per second.

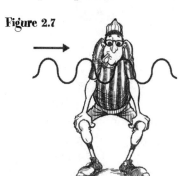

Figure 2.7

You watch as waves go by

Let's assume you have a bunch of waves that all travel at the same speed, and suppose these waves are all going past you (Figure 2.7).[2]

If someone comes by and *shortens* the wavelength of these waves, what happens to the frequency?

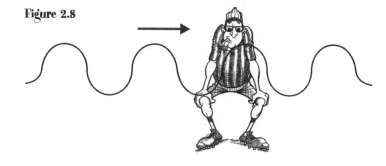

Figure 2.8

Well, with shorter wavelengths, more wavelengths pass you in a given time, so that means the frequency *increases* (Figure 2.8). By the same token, increasing the wavelength lowers the frequency. That gives us the following rule:

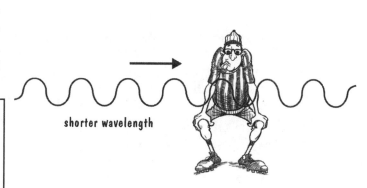

shorter wavelength

> For waves traveling at the same speed, when wavelength increases, frequency decreases. When wavelength decreases, frequency increases.

---

[1] It might be useful to think of one wavelength as the distance from one "crest" to another.

---

[2] You probably didn't, or couldn't, notice, but the waves you produced on the rope in the previous section actually did travel at the same speed, regardless of how fast you moved the end of the rope. You'll just have to trust me on that one.

What I've told you so far applies to all kinds of waves, but what does this have to do with light? Water waves and waves on a rope aren't the same as light waves, are they? Yes and no. Yes, because light waves have a frequency and wavelength associated with them, and those two things obey the relationship I talked about above. No, because light waves are caused by something other than a person moving a rope or water up and down.

Time for a short digression. Remember back when you were 18 months old and you learned about atoms and molecules? As a refresher, here's how it works. Just about everything in the world (except light!) is made of molecules, and molecules are made of itsy bitsy things called atoms. Atoms, in turn, are made of itsier bitsier things called protons, neutrons, and electrons. What might come to mind is a picture of a nucleus of protons and neutrons surrounded by electrons moving in circles around the nucleus. Never mind that such a picture is really inaccurate—it'll do for now. By the way, the electrons in our model of an atom basically have no size whatsoever, making them about the smallest little devils you can imagine. Of course, I'm saying this as if the existence of electrons is an unchangeable fact. Their existence is no such thing. Electrons are part of a scientific model, and as I said before, scientists *make up* scientific models. Those little tiny electrons that no one can see might or might not exist, and it's a sure bet you don't see them flying around. In the end, it's a matter of your philosophy of life as to whether or not electrons exist. At any rate, and here's the important point, the world behaves as if electrons *do* exist. So from here on out, we'll assume they exist.

SCI LINKS®
THE WORLD'S A CLICK AWAY

Topic: wavelength

Go to: *www.scilinks.org*

Code: SFL04

After all that, here's how to make light waves: move an electron up and down, just as you would move the end of a rope up and down (see Figure 2.9). Now that's not entirely correct, but it's pretty close to correct. Until we get to the next section at least, let's assume that the way you make light waves is to move electrons up and down (actually, sideways works, too). The faster you move them, the higher the frequency of the waves you create, just as with waves on a rope. The slower you move them, the lower the frequency of the waves you create. And of course that earlier business about frequency and wavelength applies here. Higher frequency means shorter wavelength and lower frequency means longer wavelength.

Figure 2.9

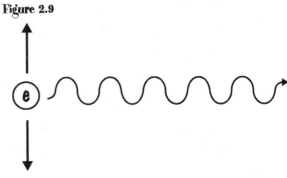

Moving an electron up and down sends out light waves

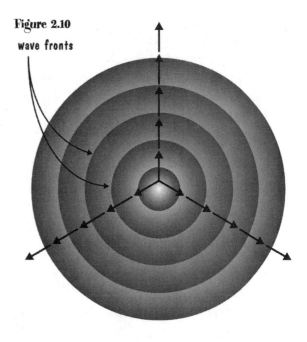

Figure 2.10

wave fronts

One final thing in this section. When you made ripple waves in the pan of water (Figure 2.10), did you notice that the wave crests formed what you might call a "front," meaning that all the wave crests created at the same time traveled outward as one?

If you didn't notice that, go back and take another look. In the last part of this chapter, I'll be explaining how refraction works, and it will help there to view light in terms of wave fronts.

Before I go on, let me make it clear that we now have two models for what light is. One is a ray model, where light travels in straight lines and only changes direction when it goes from one medium to another. The second is a wave model, where light travels in waves that have a wavelength and a frequency associated with them. Using this model, we'll be able to explain why light is able to change direction even when it doesn't change mediums. Stay tuned for that in Chapter 5. I know, you can't wait!

More things to do before you read more science stuff

This is an easy section. Search around the house for a crystal, some leaded glass, a prism, or anything that produces a rainbow when light shines through it. If you don't have anything like that around, rent the movie Pollyanna and vicariously enjoy the part where the kids hang all sorts of crystals in the window of the previously mean person's house, creating a room full of rainbows. No video store nearby? Get the "rainbow peephole" that came with this book. Look through it at any old lightbulb and say "oooh" and "aaah" as you see all the pretty colors.

More science stuff

News flash: White light is composed of all colors. You know that because prisms, crystals, and diffraction gratings[3] (that's what the rainbow peephole is) separate white light into all its component colors. Which brings up a question. What's

---

[3] I'll explain what a diffraction grating is and why it makes rainbows in Chapter 5.

the difference between different colors of light, other than the fact that they're different colors? It turns out that different colors of light have different *wavelengths*. Red light has the longest wavelength, and violet light has the shortest wavelength. Other colors have wavelengths in between these two in size. To picture this, we can draw a sort of graph of what's known as the **visible spectrum**, as in Figure 2.11.

Figure 2.11

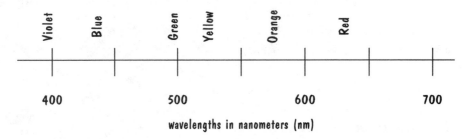

wavelengths in nanometers (nm)

The strange units that wavelengths of light are measured in are **nanometers.** One nanometer is equal to 0.000000001 meters. So a wave of red light, with a wavelength of about 650 nanometers, is 650 times 0.000000001 meters, or 0.00000065 meters long. That's tiny! So although you can see water waves and waves on a rope, there is no way you can see directly that light is made of waves.

In addition to drawing a graph that shows the wavelengths of light, we draw a graph that shows the frequencies of light. And there it is in Figure 2.12.[4]

Figure 2.12

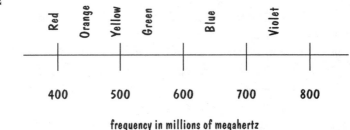

frequency in millions of megahertz

A couple of things to notice. First, red and blue have switched ends. That's because shorter wavelengths have higher frequencies, and longer wavelengths have lower frequencies. Second, we have more strange units on this graph. What in the heck is a hertz? One hertz is a unit of 1/seconds. Remember that fre-

---

[4] One way to remember the order of colors in the visible spectrum is to use the acronym ROY G. BIV, which represents red, orange, yellow, green, blue, indigo, and violet. Note that I left out indigo in the diagram.

quency is the number of wavelengths that pass a given point *per* second. That's why the unit is 1/seconds.[5] The unit is named not for a car rental company, but for physicist Heinrich Hertz.

Remember I said you can create light waves by moving an electron up and down? I also said that's not quite an accurate picture. What you get when you physically move electrons up and down are *radio waves*.[6] So what I'm going to do is describe in detail what radio waves are. After that, I'll tie that description to a description of light. Trust me; it'll all come together into one nice picture!

For starters, what do radio waves travel on? Waves on a rope travel along the rope and water waves travel on the water. In these cases, something you can touch (the rope, the water) actually moves up and down as the waves pass by. Radio waves, however, seem to magically get from that antenna up on the hill to your radio. You don't see the waves passing by as you might see water waves passing by (Figure 2.13).

Figure 2.13

How do the waves get here from the radio antenna?

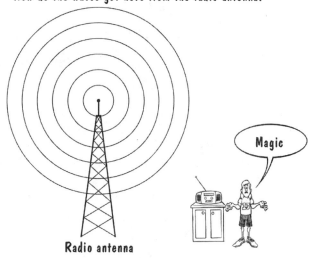

Radio antenna

Magic

The trick is that the things that move up and down (and also sideways and every other direction) are made-up, invisible things called electric fields and magnetic fields. That might come across as 'It's the fairies, silly!" but that's my story and I'm sticking to it. Seriously, charged-up things like electrons exert forces on other charged-up things, and electric and magnetic fields are part of the scientific model that physicists use to explain all that interaction.

So here's the model of radio waves. Moving an electron up and

---

[5] This might seem like an odd unit. You're probably familiar with units such as meters, seconds, or even meters per second. What does it mean to have just seconds in the denominator? The key here is that frequency is a *number* of wavelengths per second, or a *number* of vibrations per second. Those *numbers* don't have any units attached; they're just numbers. So, we end up with units only in the denominator.

[6] You don't create radio waves by holding an electron in your hand and jiggling it. Instead, you make the electrons in a wire (an antenna) move up and down by rapidly switching the direction of the thing (think battery and you'll be close) that makes the electrons move one way or the other.

down generates changing electric and magnetic fields, and these changing fields cause each other to travel through different mediums, including empty space.

Figure 2.14

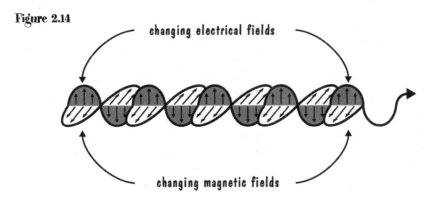

changing electrical fields

changing magnetic fields

The changing electric and magnetic fields are at right angles (perpendicular) to each other, and the overall direction of motion is perpendicular to the directions of the changing fields (Figure 2.14). Also notice that what we have is a *wave*, with a definite wavelength and of course, a definite frequency. The faster you jiggle the electrons up and down to start the radio waves, the higher the frequency and the smaller the wavelength of the radio waves. Of course, you know all about radio waves having different frequencies, as you tune your radio to pick up stations that broadcast at different frequencies.

Before moving on, let's recap. By jiggling electrons around, you can create radio waves that move along all by themselves, even in empty space. Radio waves consist of changing electric and magnetic fields, and they can have different frequencies and wavelengths. And by the way, these waves are called, not surprisingly, **electromagnetic waves.**

Electromagnetic waves are called radio waves in the frequency range of about 1 kilohertz to about 100 megahertz.[7] If you increase the frequency beyond 100 megahertz, you end up with microwaves. Yep, those same waves you use to cook your food. So the only difference between microwaves and radio waves is the frequency. Microwaves consist of changing electric and magnetic fields, just like radio waves.

Maybe you can see where this is going. If not, I'll tell you. If you increase the frequency of electromagnetic waves all the way up to around 400 million megahertz, you're at the frequency of visible light. And in fact, that is what you have—light. Light waves are electromagnetic waves, just like radio and microwaves. The only difference between light waves and other electromagnetic waves

---

[7] 1 kilohertz is equal to 1000 hertz and 1 megahertz is equal to 1000 kilohertz.

is the frequency. This leads us to a graph you've probably seen before. Figure 2.15 shows what's known as the **electromagnetic spectrum.**

Figure 2.15

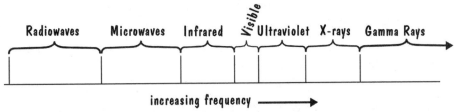

The Electromagnetic Spectrum

You might notice a few familiar names in the electromagnetic spectrum—infrared light, ultraviolet light, X rays, and gamma rays. All of these are electromagnetic waves that just differ from one another in frequency and wavelength. Also, note that visible light makes up a very small part of the electromagnetic spectrum.

I told you that all you have to do is increase the frequency of electromagnetic waves enough and you get visible light, and that's true. However, by the time you get to the frequency of visible light, the notion of jiggling electrons around, or even doing the equivalent of having them go around in circles really fast, totally breaks down. The electromagnetic waves that are produced act as if jiggling electrons made them, but for reasons that go beyond the scope of this book, physicists are quite certain that's not what the electrons are doing when they produce light. I'll give you sort of a vague idea of what they *are* doing in the last chapter of this book.

Even more things to do before you read even more science stuff

Now that we have a model of what light waves are, we're ready to look at what happens when you combine paints, filters, and different-colored lights to produce new colors. The explanation will involve how light waves interact with matter.

SCI LINKS.
THE WORLD'S A CLICK AWAY

Topic: electromagnetic spectrum

Go to: *www.scilinks.org*

Code: SFL05

Three different-colored filters came with this book. Get 'em and look through them at all sorts of different colored objects. You should notice a few odd things, such as the fact that blue objects look black when you look at them through a red filter. Why do you suppose that happens?

If you can't figure that one out, then try a simpler question. Forget about looking through filters—why is any object the color it is? What makes red things red, green things green, and fuchsia things fuchsia?

While you're pondering that question, try holding combinations of filters up to the light. You know, use blue and yellow to make green, and stuff like that. Takes you right back to fourth grade art class, huh? What do you think causes you to see the new colors? What happens when you put red and blue together? Were you expecting purple?[8]

Get various paint colors (your kid's watercolors will do) and combine different colors to create new ones. Compare the colors you get mixing paints with the colors you get looking at a light source through combinations of filters.

And now for something completely different.[9] Find a friend and three flashlights. Tape one colored filter, or gel, to each of the flashlights so they produce red, blue, and yellow light. With your friend's help, shine various combinations of light onto a white sheet of paper (Figure 2.16).

Check out all possible combinations of two colors, and then shine all three of them on the spot at once (here's where you need your friend). Notice how yellow and blue make green, just as before. Er, well—no they don't.

Figure 2.16

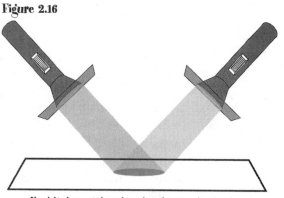

flashlights with colored gels taped over front

Even more science stuff

With a ray model of light, we thought of light as either bouncing off something (reflection) or traveling right on through a substance and possibly refracting. In order to explain what you just observed, however, I'm going to give you a different view of what's going on when light interacts with matter.[10] Picture an object as being composed of tiny little atoms, with each atom con-

---

[8] When you put together the red and blue filters that come with this book, you might convince yourself that you see a very dark purple. Then again, it might just look black.

[9] Apologies to Monty Python.

[10] What I mean by "matter" is any kind of material—water, a mirror, a rock, a leather jacket, a piece of glass, or whatever.

taining electrons. Now, just as electrons can create light waves, when light waves run into electrons, it's possible for those light waves to cause the electrons to do something. For now, we'll stick with that incorrect idea that the electrons jiggle around. In general, there will be some kind of interaction between the incoming light and the electrons in the atoms of the object. In fact, what happens is that the atoms *absorb* and then *reradiate* the incoming light (Figure 2.17).

When they reradiate the light, they don't always reradiate the same frequency as the incoming light. And actually that's all you need to know to understand why different objects are different colors. Suppose you have a yellow shirt on. White light (containing all colors) hits your shirt. The atoms in your shirt are such that they absorb all the frequencies of light and then reradiate

Figure 2.17

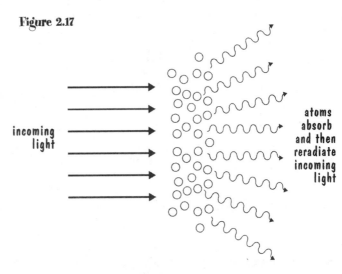

incoming light

atoms absorb and then reradiate incoming light

only the frequencies corresponding to yellow light (Figure 2.18).

At this point, you might be wondering why a yellow cotton shirt reradiates different colors from a blue cotton shirt. After all, they're made of the same material. The answer is in the dye used to color the shirts. The molecules in yellow dye are structurally different from the molecules in blue dye, so they react differently to the incoming light and reradiate different frequencies of that light.

Figure 2.18

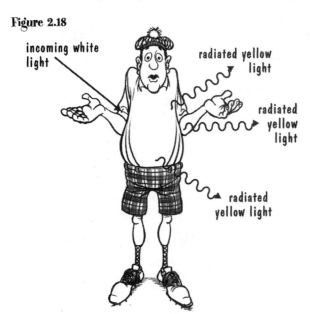

incoming white light

radiated yellow light

radiated yellow light

radiated yellow light

It's a short step from this to figuring out how filters work. When light hits a filter, that filter absorbs all but a certain range of frequencies,

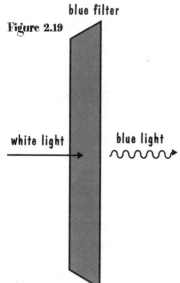

Figure 2.19

blue filter

white light → blue light 〰️→

and that certain range passes on through the filter (Figure 2.19).[11]

We can represent this process with a graph that shows how much of each frequency different colors of light contain. For example, Figure 2.20 shows this graph for white light. It contains all the colors (all the visible frequencies) plus probably some infrared and ultraviolet light, which is why the graph looks the way it does.

Figure 2.20

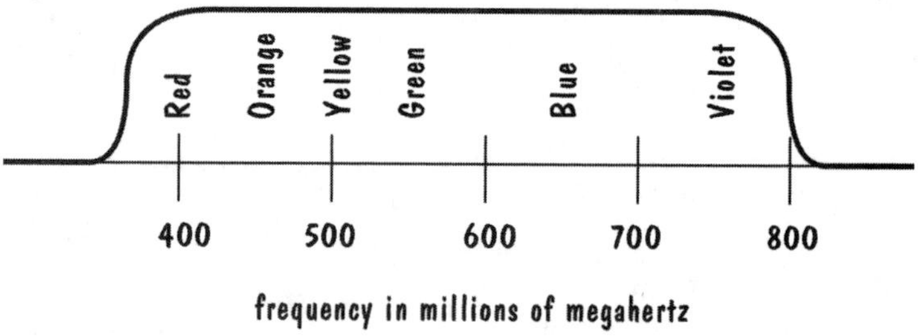

Red Orange Yellow Green Blue Violet

400   500   600   700   800

frequency in millions of megahertz

Now let's draw this same kind of graph for the light that makes it through the blue filter (Figure 2.21).

Notice that this filter doesn't let just blue light through. There's some green and violet light in there, too.[12] Even though those other colors make it through the filter, the light still looks blue to us. Figure 2.22 shows similar graphs for

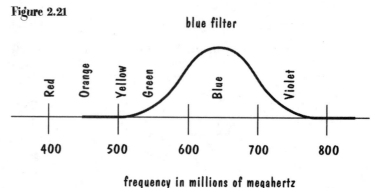

Figure 2.21

blue filter

Red Orange Yellow Green Blue Violet

400   500   600   700   800

frequency in millions of megahertz

---

[11] Technically, the light that makes it through a filter is reradiated light, but it's convenient to think of this light as just passing through the filter.

---

[12] By the way, you *could* make a filter that only lets the frequencies corresponding to blue light pass, but that filter would be too expensive to include with this book!

light that passes through a red filter and light that passes through a yellow filter.

Figure 2.22

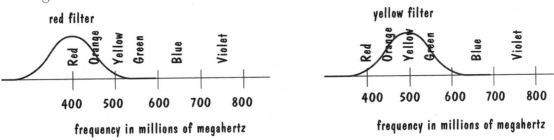

red filter

frequency in millions of megahertz

yellow filter

frequency in millions of megahertz

One way to look at what filters do is to say they *subtract* from the incoming light. A red filter takes white light and *subtracts out* all frequencies but those shown in Figure 2.22.

Okay, why does a blue object look black when you look at it through a red filter? Just look at the frequency graphs in Figures 2.23 and 2.24.

The red filter only allows the frequencies on the left to pass through it, and the blue object only emits the frequencies on the right. There's no overlap, meaning *none* of the blue light from the object gets through the red filter. No light means the object looks black. Similarly, red objects look black when you view them through a blue filter.

Let's move on to combinations of filters. What happens when you look through both a yellow and a blue filter? Again, look at the frequency graphs.

The only light that makes it through both filters is the light in the region of overlap. And guess what? Those are the

Figure 2.23

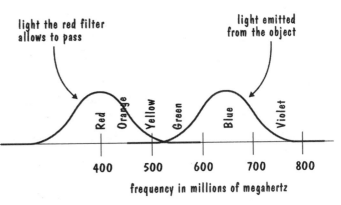

light the red filter allows to pass

light emitted from the object

frequency in millions of megahertz

Figure 2.24

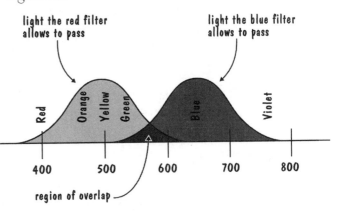

light the red filter allows to pass

light the blue filter allows to pass

region of overlap

frequencies that correspond to green light! Simple, huh? You can use this same reasoning to figure out why a combination of red and yellow filters gives you orange light.[13] But what about red and blue together? They're supposed to make purple, right? No, not always. With a red and blue filter, you have the frequency graph shown in Figure 2.25. There's virtually no overlap at all, so no light makes it through both filters.[14]

Figure 2.25

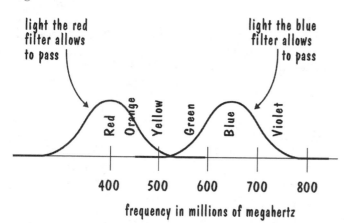

light the red filter allows to pass

light the blue filter allows to pass

Red Orange Yellow Green Blue Violet

400   500   600   700   800

frequency in millions of megahertz

Okay, if that's true, then why can you mix red and blue paints to get purple? Actually, if you mix a dark blue paint with a dark red paint, you will pretty much get black instead of purple. To get a nice purple color, you need to mix some white paint in with the red and blue, and that makes for a much more complicated situation than just putting a red and blue filter together.

Let's stop here and realize that the two processes—combining filters and mixing paints—give essentially the same results. Both processes are examples of *color subtraction*. Both filters and paints absorb certain frequencies of light (that's the subtraction) and reradiate others. With color subtraction, combining blue and yellow produces green.

So now we're set. We know what always happens when you add the colors red, yellow, and blue, right? Nope. Remember that when you used flashlights to shine blue and yellow light on a single spot on white paper, you *didn't* end up with green. That means combining blue and yellow doesn't always give you green. The key to understanding this is that when you shine two lights on a single spot, you are *adding* the separate frequencies of light (Figure 2.26).

[13] The yellow filter that came with this book actually lets through quite a bit of red light. Therefore, combining the red and yellow filters gives you more of a reddish orange than a pure orange color.

[14] The red filter that came with this book actually lets a tiny bit of violet light through, so instead of black you might see a very dark purple color.

Figure 2.26

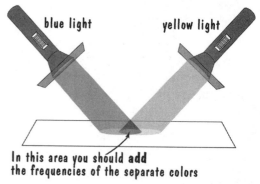

blue light   yellow light

In this area you should **add** the frequencies of the separate colors

Let's take a look at this using the frequency graphs. As before, we have the separate graphs for blue and yellow in Figure 2.27.

Because we're adding light instead of subtracting light, we *add* in the places where the two graphs overlap. The result is in Figure 2.28.

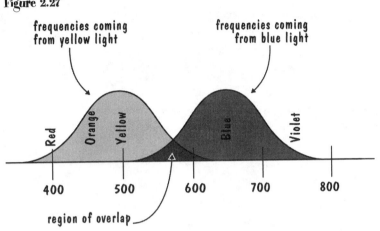

Figure 2.27

frequencies coming from yellow light

frequencies coming from blue light

region of overlap

You can see that by adding these frequencies, we get something closer to white light (all frequencies) than we had before. The only frequencies missing are the reds and a little bit of orange. That's why you see a washed out area where the beams overlap, instead of the color green. If you add a third flashlight to shine red light on the same spot, you will end up with a white spot.

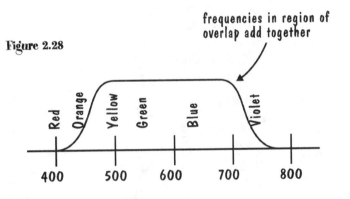

Figure 2.28

frequencies in region of overlap add together

To sum up, color subtraction produces new colors by *removing* frequencies of light. Color addition produces new colors by *adding* separate frequencies of light.

And even more things to do before you read even more science stuff

Right about now, you're undoubtedly thinking to yourself, "Sure, that's fine finding out about the electromagnetic spectrum and how filters work, but what causes rainbows and why is the sky blue?" Thought you'd never ask. As usual, before I give you the answers, you have to do a couple of things.

Go outside when the Sun is shining, and when it's relatively low in the sky (avoid the hours between ten and two, unless you live in Alaska and the Sun is always low in the sky). Grab a garden hose with a spray attachment and make sure the hose is connected to a faucet. Stand with the Sun at your back and spray water in front of you (Figure 2.29).

Figure 2.29

"I'm...melting...you wretched neighbor!... But, look at that pretty rainbow..."

You should see a rainbow in the spray of water. If not, reposition the spray until you do.

Now head back inside and find a large, clear bowl. Fill it with water and nab a flashlight and some milk (Figure 2.30). Set up the bowl so you can shine the flashlight through it and see the spot it makes on a wall on the other side of the bowl.

Figure 2.30

Begin adding drops of milk to the water. As you do, notice two things: a) the color the bowl of water appears to be when you look at it from the side and b) the color of the spot on the wall. Keep adding drops of milk until the bowl of water is a definite blue color and the spot on the wall is red. Neat, huh?

And even more science stuff

Before I get to rainbows and blue sky, I'm going to use a wave model to explain refraction, as I promised in Chapter 1. Remember that when light interacts with matter, the atoms and molecules in the matter absorb and reradiate the light. This is true even when light passes through something clear like glass. All this absorption and reradiation takes time, which means that light slows down when it travels through matter. The denser the medium, the slower light moves through it. As an aside, the fastest light moves is when it's traveling though empty space, or a vacuum. In that case, we let *c* represent the speed of light; *c* has a value of 300,000,000 meters per second, or 186,000 miles per second.[15]

Now let's look at what happens when light waves travel from air into a block of glass. We're going to look at light as traveling in *wave fronts*.

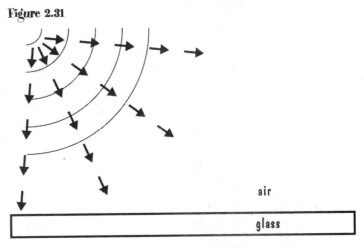

Figure 2.31

air

glass

A bunch of wave fronts headed toward a block of glass

When these wave fronts hit the glass, they're going to move more slowly because glass is denser than air. To figure out what that means for the waves, pretend these wave fronts are lines of people in a marching band.[16] Also pretend the air is a dry field and the glass is a muddy field. When the people in the band reach the mud, they'll slow down. What's going to happen in Figure 2.31 then, is that the bottom part of each wave front (line of people) is going to reach the glass (muddy field) before the upper part. As each successive part of the wave front (line

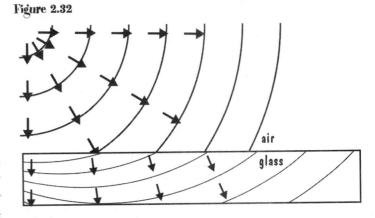

Figure 2.32

air

glass

of people) reaches the glass (muddy field), it in turn slows down. The result is that the wave front (line of people) bends as shown in Figure 2.32.

So that's how refraction comes about. It's because light waves travel at different speeds in different mediums. To take this further, different frequencies of light slow down different amounts when they hit a denser medium. That means they refract different amounts when they hit a denser medium. And that means

[15] This is pretty darned fast. Light can travel about seven times around the Earth in a single second.

[16] To keep things simple, let's assume we're talking about light of a single frequency.

that when white light hits a block of glass, the different colors spread out. That's why a prism breaks white light into its component colors. Pink Floyd made a valiant attempt to help the world discover this fact with the cover art on *Dark Side of the Moon*.

Figure 2.33

"I could tell you...if I only had a book on 'light'."

On to rainbows. To figure out those, let's look at what happens when sunlight hits a drop of water. If the sunlight, water drop, and you are all in just the right positions, here's what will happen: light refracts as it enters the water drop, and the colors separate as they travel through the drop. When the light hits the back of the drop, at least some of it reflects as shown in Figure 2.34 and travels back through the drop to you.

Finally, I'll explain the light and milky water setup. Different-sized molecules tend to absorb and reradiate some frequencies more than others. Milk molecules are particularly good at absorbing and reradiating blue light, and the reradiated light tends

Figure 2.34

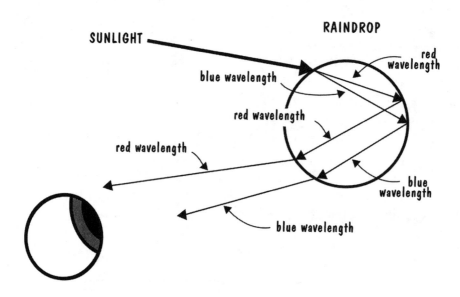

to be in a plane that is perpendicular to the direction of the incoming light. So when white light hits the milk molecules, they absorb and reradiate the blue part of the spectrum out to the side.

As you add more and more milk to the water in the bowl, more and more blue light is scattered to the side, and the liquid looks blue. Because much of the blue light is scattered to the side and removed from the flashlight beam, the spot on the wall gets redder and redder (see Figure 2.35).

This same process occurs in the Earth's atmosphere as shown in Figure 2.36. Sunlight hits tiny molecules in the atmosphere, and, like the milk molecules in the water, these molecules scatter blue light off to the sides, making the sky appear blue.[17]

This also explains red sunsets, as shown in Figure 2.37. The molecules in the atmosphere scatter blue light off to the sides, leaving primarily red light to travel on through to the viewer. Any clouds or smoke between you and the Sun enhance this effect. The reason this happens at sunrise and sunset and not midday is that when you view the Sun as it's going up or going down, you view it through a larger section of atmosphere than at midday.

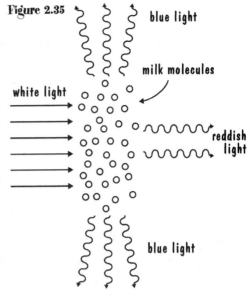

Figure 2.35

blue light

milk molecules

white light

reddish light

blue light

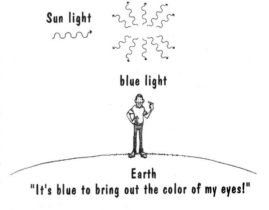

Figure 2.36   Why is the sky blue?

Sun light

blue light

Earth

"It's blue to bring out the color of my eyes!"

Figure 2.37   Why are sunsets sometimes red?

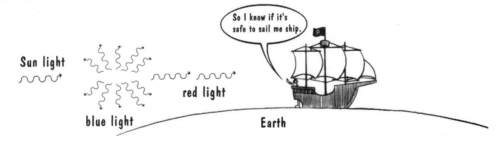

So I know if it's safe to sail me ship.

Sun light

red light

blue light

Earth

---

[17] For the record, this is known as Rayleigh scattering.

Chapter Summary

- In addition to being viewed as rays, light can be modeled as a series of waves. These waves consist of changing electric and magnetic fields that can travel through empty space, as well as through other mediums.

- The wavelength of a wave is the distance in which the wave repeats itself. The frequency of a wave is the number of wavelengths that pass a given point in a second. An increase in wavelength means a decrease in frequency, and vice versa.

- Different frequencies of light waves correspond to different colors of light. White light is composed of all the colors of visible light. Visible light is just a small portion of the entire spectrum of electromagnetic waves.

- When light interacts with matter, it is usually absorbed and then reradiated. The exact nature of the reradiated light accounts for objects being different colors and accounts for how different frequencies of light refract differently.

Applications

1. Did you ever have a game where you had to slip cards into a sleeve with a red window in order to read what's on the card? If so, today is your lucky day because I'm going to show you how those work. First find a red pencil and a blue pencil (raid your kids' stash of colored pencils). Write your name, or anything else you want, with the blue pencil on a white sheet of paper. Now use the red pencil to write a whole bunch of letters and numbers over the top of your name until you can no longer read what's written in blue.

Now look at this mess through the red filter that came with this book. Magic? Nah, just science. The red filter only allows red light to pass through it. Therefore, the white paper and the letters and numbers you wrote over your name all look red. The blue writing, however, looks black because the filter won't allow blue light to pass. You end up with black writing against a red background, which is pretty easy to see.

I can see clearly now, the red is gone.

2. Turn on your television set and look closely at the screen using a magnifying glass. You should be able to see that the screen is full of very small lines of blue, red, and green.[18] What's up with that? Well, your television actually produces only those colors. Using just those colors of light and *color addition,* the set produces every color possible. This is just like what you can do with three separate flashlights and colored filters. The separate colors on the screen are so tiny that your eye blends them all together.

3. If you've ever mixed paints, you know that paint mixing is a *color subtraction* process, because mixing yellow and blue gives you green. This color subtraction comes about because each color of paint absorbs all the frequencies of light except a limited range that corresponds to its color. It's just like stacking filters on top of each other. There is one kind of painting, though, that uses both color subtraction and color addition. In *pointillism,* the painter paints lots and lots of tiny dots of different colors. When you're close to the painting, you can see the dots, but when you're far away, your eye blends the colors, adding them to form new colors. What appears black or brown from a distance actually has no black or brown in it. Check out the paintings of Georges Seurat, and if you can get your hands on a video of the Broadway play *Sunday in the Park with George,* watch it and cry.

Topic: light and color

Go to: *www.scilinks.org*

Code: SFL06

Topic: dispersion of light

Go to: *www.scilinks.org*

Code: SFL07

---

[18] The generally accepted "primary colors" for color addition are blue, red, and green. The reason I included blue, red, and *yellow* filters with this book is so I could draw a clear distinction between color subtraction (in which blue and yellow combine to make green) and color addition (in which blue and yellow combined do not produce green).

Focus, People, Focus!

It's time to take some of the things we know about light and put them to good use. In this chapter, I'll discuss various optical instruments like antennae and lenses, and in the Applications section, you get to learn how telescopes work. That's just too darned exciting, isn't it? In case you're wondering what the heck this chapter title refers to, it's a phrase theater directors are often heard saying, and you'll understand what it has to do with the material in the chapter once you've read it.

"Focus, people! Focus!"

Things to do before you read the science stuff

Find a large bowl (if you have a wok, even better) and line the inside of it with aluminum foil (Figure 3.1). Make sure the shiny side is facing out and do what you can to smooth any wrinkles.

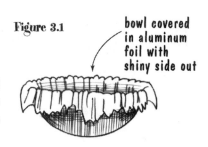

Figure 3.1

bowl covered in aluminum foil with shiny side out

Take this outside on a sunny day and hold the bowl so the inside of it faces the Sun, as shown in Figure 3.2.

Now, while holding the bowl towards the Sun and being careful not to block sunlight from hitting the foil, place your finger at various places on the inside of the bowl. I'm not talking about touching the aluminum foil but rather exploring the entire space where water would be if you filled the bowl with water. See if you can find one spot that's warmer than all the others.

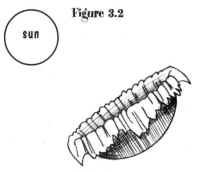

Figure 3.2

sun

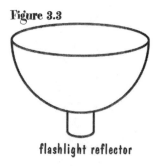

Figure 3.3

flashlight reflector

Head back inside, get one of those flashlights you've been using, and take it apart. Actually, you don't have to take it apart completely—just do what you have to do to remove the shiny reflecting part, shown in Figure 3.3.

Notice any similarity between this reflector and your foil-covered bowl? You should. Now put the flashlight back together and notice where the flashlight bulb is in relationship to the reflector. Compare this position with the position of the "hot spot" in your foil-covered bowl or wok.

The science stuff

If you were careful about feeling around for the warmest spot inside the foil-covered bowl, you probably found that spot somewhere near what is shown in Figure 3.4.

Why should it feel hotter there than anywhere else? First you need to realize that sunlight doesn't just contain visible light. It also contains infrared and ultraviolet light. Infrared light is radiated heat—the stuff that makes you feel warm when you stand in the sun. This means that the spot in Figure 3.4 must be a

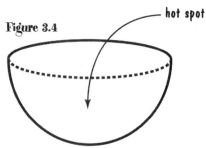

Figure 3.4

hot spot

place where you get hit with more than your usual amount of infrared light. To see why this is, all we have to do is figure out what happens to *any* electromagnetic waves that hit the bowl. We can use a simple ray diagram to do that. Figure 3.5 shows light from the Sun hitting the bowl. Because the Sun is so far away, the light that hits the bowl is essentially all moving in the same direction and the incoming rays are parallel to one another. These parallel rays hit the sides of the bowl and reflect off.

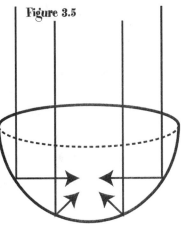

Figure 3.5

Because the bowl is curved (as most bowls are), the incoming light rays all get reflected into the center of the bowl. This concentration of light, which includes infrared light, makes for a hot spot (Figure 3.5).

Figure 3.6

A bowl doesn't really send all the incoming light rays to one point. In order to accomplish that, you need a special shape known as a **parabola**.[1] With a parabolic shape, all the incoming light would reflect exactly to one special spot known as the **focus** of the parabola[2] (Figure 3.6).

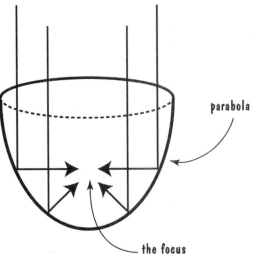

parabola

the focus

A wok is actually much closer to being parabolic (this is by design, so food that hits the sides is directed towards the middle of the wok), so it will produce a warmer hot spot than will a bowl.

Aside from the fact that you've got a great start on a solar cooker (place a marshmallow at the focus and see what happens), what good is all this? Well, take a look at microwave antennae, satellite dishes, and large radio telescopes (look these up on the Internet). They're all parabolas, designed to take incoming electromagnetic waves and concentrate them in a single spot (the focus).

---

[1] Parabolas can be wide or narrow, tall or short. Their shape is determined by a specific mathematical-geometrical relationship, and it's not always obvious from looking whether or not a given shape is a parabola. It's a pretty sure bet that your average kitchen bowl is *not* a parabola.

---

[2] Stupid joke time. The mother named the family cattle ranch "Focus" because it's the place where her sons raise meat. Okay, I'll explain it. If you aim a parabolic reflector at the Sun, the Sun's rays will meet at the focus of the parabola. Therefore, the focus is where the Sun's rays meet. Told you it was stupid!

Figure 3.7

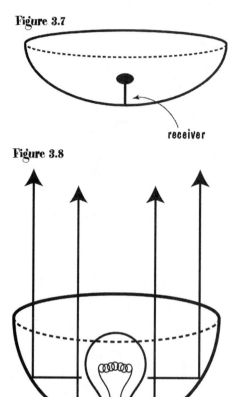

receiver

Figure 3.8

Place your receiver at the focus and you're in business, as shown in Figure 3.7.

All right, what about the flashlight? You don't use flashlights to collect electromagnetic waves but you do use them to send out electromagnetic waves. A flashlight reflector just does the reverse of what our foil-covered bowl did. Light that leaves the focus of a parabola hits the sides and leaves as parallel rays, as in Figure 3.8.

Place the flashlight bulb at the focus of the reflector, and you send out light in a set of more-or-less parallel rays. Of course, some flashlights are better than others. Cheap flashlights have reflectors that aren't parabolic and have bulbs that aren't exactly at the focus of the reflector.

To go beyond flashlights, you can obviously send out any kind of electromagnetic waves using a parabolic reflector. All you have to do is put the source of those waves at the focus, and turn it on. What this means is that a microwave transmitter looks exactly like a microwave receiver.

More things to do before you read more science stuff

Get an empty toilet paper tube, a small sheet of construction paper (any color), a small sheet of waxed paper, and a couple of rubber bands. Use the rubber bands to place the construction paper and waxed paper over the ends of the

Figure 3.9

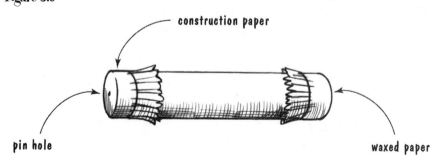

construction paper

pin hole

waxed paper

tube, as shown in Figure 3.9. Use a pin to poke a tiny hole in the center of the construction paper side of the tube.

Figure 3.10

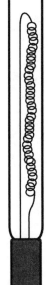

Now find a light source. A regular lightbulb will do, and so will a candle flame (be careful with this one, though!), but the best thing to use is a long, tube-shaped lightbulb like the one in Figure 3.10. You can get a 25-watt bulb that will fit into a normal socket at most any store for less than two bucks, and I'm going to ask you to get one of these in Chapter 5, so why not get one now?

With your light source on, hold the tube so the construction paper side (with the pinhole) faces the light. Look at the waxed paper side of the tube as you move the tube around a bit. Also move the tube toward and away from the light source and see what happens (Figure 3.11).

Figure 3.11

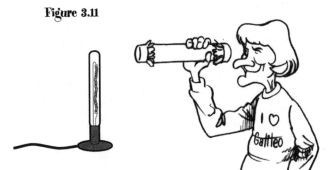

You should get a pretty clear image on the waxed paper of the filament of the bulb if the bulb is transparent, the entire bulb if the bulb is frosted, or the flame. Notice anything strange about the image? How does the image change when you move the tube back and forth and side to side?

More science stuff

What you just made is known as a **pinhole camera,** which makes sense because it has a pinhole in it! We can use a ray diagram to see how it works, and why the image you saw was upside down. The light source sends light rays out in all directions, but only a tiny portion of those light rays make it through the pinhole. Figure 3.12 shows a couple of those rays, one from the top of the light source and one from the bottom. As they go through the pinhole, these rays cross, leading to an upside-down image.

Figure 3.12

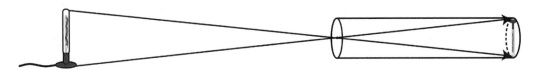

Similar diagrams in Figure 3.13 show why the image gets larger or smaller as you move the tube towards or away from the light source.

Figure 3.13

large image

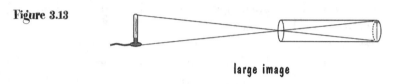

small image

If you were to place a sheet of photographic film where the waxed paper is, you could use this tube to actually take a picture of the light source. In fact, most cameras don't operate much differently from your pinhole camera. All you need to do is add a lens. Before you do that, though, maybe we should figure out how lenses work.

Even more things to do before you read even more science stuff

Find the flashlight and index card contraption you used so much in Chapter 1. Get a clear glass and fill it with water and then find a way to darken the room slightly. Turning off the lights sometimes works. Set the glass of water on a table and shine your narrow light beam through the water. Start at one side of the glass and move across to the other side. As you do this, observe what happens to the light beam that emerges from the other side of the glass (Figure 3.14).

Figure 3.14

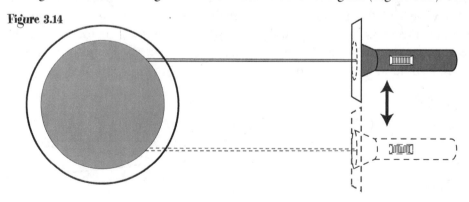

If you have a magnifying glass around (one of those cheapo plastic ones will work), get it. Shine the light beam through the magnifying glass, moving it from one side to the other as you did with the glass of water. Again notice what happens to the emerging light beam. Next take your magnifying glass outside on a sunny day and hold it just above the ground so you get a really bright spot on the ground. Takes you right back to burning ants when you were a kid, huh?[3] By the way, why is that spot so hot?

Take your magnifying glass, along with a sheet of white paper, and find a lit lightbulb. Set things up as in Figure 3.15 and move the magnifying glass varying distances from the paper until you get a clear image of the lightbulb on the paper. Cool, no? You can also do this with a television set or computer screen (in place of the lightbulb, not the magnifying glass) in a darkened room.

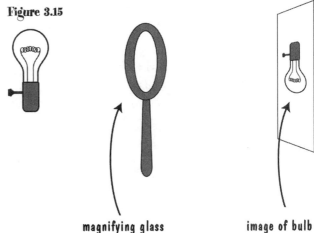

Figure 3.15

magnifying glass   image of bulb

Now look through the magnifying glass at a bunch of objects. Try holding it close to your eye and then moving it out to arm's length. Any change in what you see? Do objects appear right side up or upside down? Does it matter whether you're looking at nearby objects or faraway objects?

If you don't have a magnifying glass, fill your glass of water all the way to the top, put your hand over the top, and then hold it as shown in Figure 3.16.

Do all of the things I asked you to do with the magnifying glass. Of course, you might want to do this over a sink if your hand isn't exactly doing a great job of keeping the water in the glass. Also, you'll have a tough time forming an image of a lightbulb on a piece of paper with the glass of water.

Figure 3.16

---

[3] For the record, I'm not advocating the burning of ants! Let's just say some of us were less than angels back in the third grade.

Even more science stuff

Light beams that travel through a glass of water or a magnifying glass do some pretty serious refracting. You probably got results something like those in Figure 3.17.

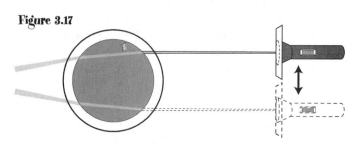

Figure 3.17

We could figure out why the light did what it did by using a ray diagram and Snell's law, but there's an easier way to think about what's happening. Instead of picturing the light as a bunch of rays, let's picture it as a series of wave fronts coming towards the magnifying glass. I'll only have to explain the magnifying glass, because the glass of water works the same way. Also, I'll get a bit more general and talk about what light does when it comes in contact with a **lens,** which is basically what a magnifying glass is. So anyway, the wave-front diagram is shown in Figure 3.18.

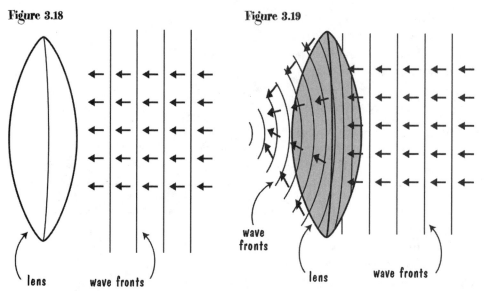

Figure 3.18

Figure 3.19

Remember that light travels more slowly in glass than it does in air and notice that the middle part of each wave front hits the lens before the other parts of the wave front. Because the middle of the lens is thicker than the ends, the middle of the wave will spend more time at a slower speed, and it will fall behind the other parts of the wave. The result is that each wave front curves as shown in Figure 3.19 and converges to a point on the other side of the lens.

To get a feel for what each wave front is going through, pretend you're a wave front by walking along with your arms straight over your head. Now make your stomach "fall behind" your arms and legs. Your body now has the shape of a converging wave front (Figure 3.20).

Figure 3.20

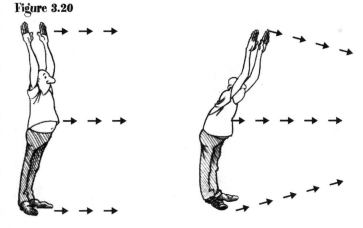

Back to the lens. The point at which the incoming wave fronts, which correspond to parallel light rays, converge is called the **focal point** of the lens. When you used the magnifying glass to make a bright spot using sunlight, that spot was the focal point of the magnifying glass, and the distance between the glass and the spot was the focal length of the lens. A lens that's shaped like the one in Figure 3.18 is called a **converging,** or **convex** lens.

Now let's look at what might happen with a different shaped lens, in particular the one shown in Figure 3.21. In this case, the center of the wave front travels longer in air, and therefore gets *ahead* of the rest of the wave (your stomach jumps ahead of your arms and legs, which for many of us is sort of the normal way of things anyway!), and the wave front *diverges* away from the lens. Not surprisingly, this kind of lens is called a **diverging,** or **concave** lens.

Figure 3.21

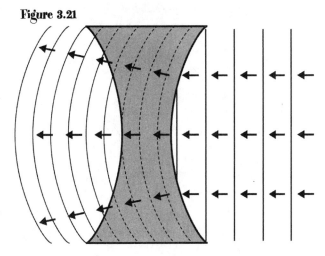

Convex and concave lenses are useful for all sorts of things, not the least of which is for eyeglasses or contact lenses. I'll address those useful things in Chapter 6. In the meantime, I promised I'd explain telescopes in the Applications section, so we better get moving in that direction. To do that, I need to explain why you saw things the way you did when looking through the magnifying glass or the glass of water.

Again, I'm just going to use a basic convex lens to make things simple. What applies to this lens also applies to the magnifying glass and approximately to the

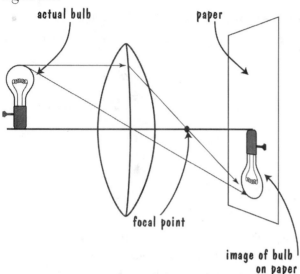

Figure 3.22

actual bulb | paper

focal point

image of bulb on paper

glass of water. Let's start with forming an image of a light bulb on a sheet of paper. Figure 3.22 shows that setup.

I've drawn two light rays that leave the top of the bulb. One hits the lens as a parallel ray, and as we now know, that ray will refract and go through the focal point of the lens.[4] Another ray goes through the center of the lens. That ray pretty much passes straight on through without refracting (you're just going to have to trust me on that!). Notice that those two rays intersect on the other side of the lens where we've placed the paper. I'm not going to go into detail, but if you trace every other ray that leaves the top of the light bulb and goes through the lens, they will all end up at that intersection point on the paper. This means that there will be an image of the top of the bulb at that point. If we follow that ray-tracing process for all parts of the bulb, we'll get the entire image of the bulb that's shown in Figure 3.22. Notice that the image is upside down, as it is when you actually do this.

It's a short step to figure out what kind of image you see when you look at a faraway object while holding the lens away from your eye at least half an arm's length. All we do is remove the sheet of paper from Figure 3.22 so the light rays can continue on

Figure 3.23

image of actual bulb | where paper used to be

focal point

these rays appear to be coming from this image

[4] I just chose an arbitrary location for the focal points in Figures 3.22 and 3.24, so don't go nuts trying to figure out why they are where they are.

after they intersect (Figure 3.23). When you see these rays, they look like they're coming from an image that's where the paper used to be. So you see an upside-down image of the bulb.[5]

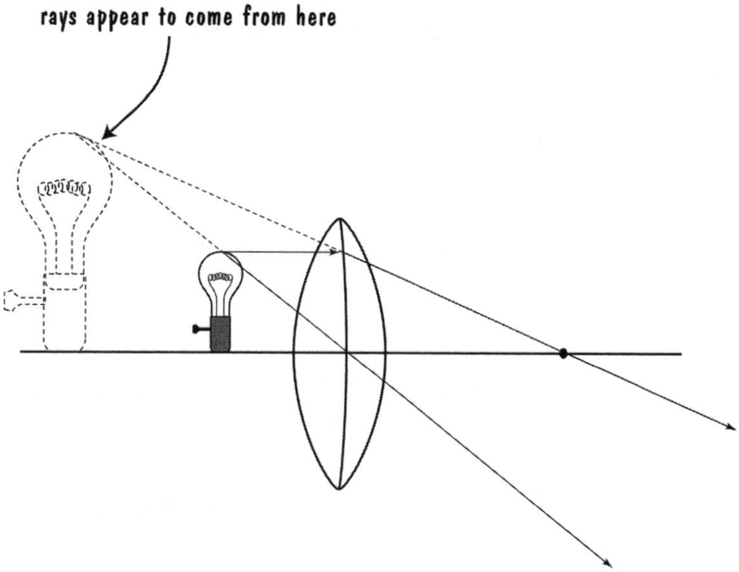

Finally, here's how a lens can magnify an image when the image is close to the lens. Figure 3.24 shows this situation and it also shows the same kind of rays I drew in Figure 3.22—one that comes into the lens as a parallel ray and refracts through the focal point and one that goes through the center of the lens and doesn't refract.

This time the two rays don't intersect on the other side of the lens. They do, however, appear to be coming from the image shown in Figure 3.25. The image appears to be much larger than the real object, so we have a magnification. Maybe that's why they call them magnifying glasses!

Figure 3.24

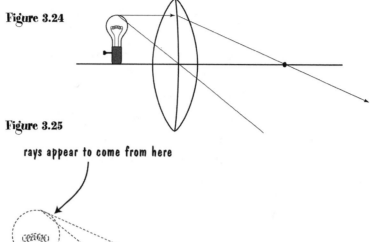

Figure 3.25

rays appear to come from here

That's as far as I'm going to take you with lenses and such, as we've covered the basics. If you pick up a physics text and find the chapter on *geometrical optics*, you'll see diagrams similar to those on the previous pages. You'll also see lots of equations that one can use to determine exactly the location and size of images formed by lenses and mirrors. Suffice it to say that, if you plan on building a microscope or other optical instrument, you'd better use those equations.

---

[5] If this isn't making any sense, go back and review the material in Chapter 1 where I discuss how we see images where the light *appears* to be coming from.

Chapter Summary

- When sending and receiving electromagnetic waves (light, radio waves, microwaves), a parabolic reflector can direct waves to and from a focal point, enhancing the reception or transmission.

- Lenses, used alone or in combinations, enable us to see images of objects that are magnified, reduced, projected, or otherwise altered.

- Lenses that cause light waves to converge are called convex lenses, and lenses that cause light waves to diverge are called concave lenses.

- To determine where a series of lenses and other optical instruments will form an image, you trace what happens to the rays of light emitted by the object being viewed.

Applications

1. Now we get to telescopes. Figure 3.26 shows two kinds of telescopes—a refracting telescope and a reflecting telescope. Not surprisingly, the refracting telescope uses two lenses while the reflecting telescope uses mirrors and a lens.

Figure 3.26

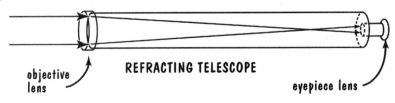

objective lens   **REFRACTING TELESCOPE**   eyepiece lens

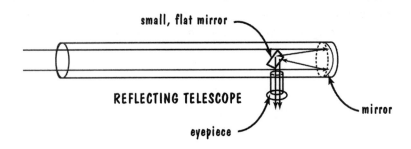

small, flat mirror

REFLECTING TELESCOPE   mirror

eyepiece

First the refracting telescope. There are two main lenses. One is a really large lens, known as the **objective.** The objective gathers light from distant objects such as planets and stars and forms an image of them inside the telescope. This works just like using a magnifying glass to look at distant objects. The bigger the objective, the more light it can gather, and the better the telescope. However, no matter what size the objective, the image it forms is rather small. To get a larger image, there's a second lens called the **eyepiece.** This lens magnifies the image formed by the objective so you can see it better. The eyepiece works just like using a magnifying glass to look at something that's close to the magnifying lens.

So telescopes are pretty simple. The larger they are, the more light they can gather, and the better images you get. There's a problem with refracting telescopes, though. The larger the objective lens, the heavier it is, not to mention being much more expensive to make. The lens can get so large it sags under its own weight. To remedy that, we move to reflecting telescopes, which use a large parabolic mirror in place of the objective lens. This mirror gathers the light and sends it to a tiny mirror that's at the focus of the parabolic mirror. The image formed by this combination is once again pretty small, so we need an eyepiece lens to magnify it. There are two nice things about reflecting telescopes. First, large mirrors are cheaper to make than large lenses. Second, the mirror is at the bottom of the reflecting telescope, so you can support it underneath and keep it from sagging under its own weight. This means you can make a much larger reflecting telescope than you can a refracting tele-scope. Most major tele-scopes these days, includ-ing the Hubble Space Telescope, are reflecting telescopes.

2. Binoculars are nothing but a couple of miniature telescopes. They work exactly the same as a re-fracting telescope but they use prisms to cause the incoming light to un-dergo total internal re-flection in getting to the eyepieces. (See Figure 3.27.) This redirection of the light is necessary in

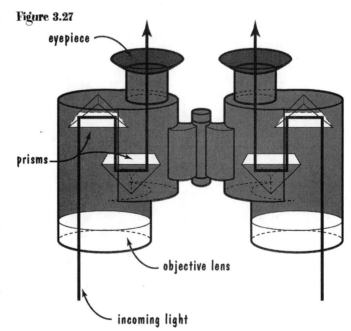

Figure 3.27

eyepiece

prisms

objective lens

incoming light

order to get the light from very large objective lenses to the eyepieces, which can't be farther apart than our eyes!

3. Cameras operate basically like the pinhole camera you made but with lenses added to get a brighter and sharper image. If the camera has a single lens, you can't zoom in and out and your picture taking is limited. If the camera has two lenses, though, you can change the position between the two lenses and change the size of the image the camera creates. In other words, modern cameras are telescopes with film added!

Topic: lenses

Go to: *www.scilinks.org*

Code: SFL08

Not-So-Cheap Sunglasses

If you browse through the sunglasses at your local department store, you'll find that some of them are advertised as "polarized." What is it that makes a pair of polarized sunglasses so special, and are they really better at reducing glare, as advertised? To answer those questions, you have to understand what **polarized light** is. Lucky for you, this chapter is all about polarized light!

Things to do before you read the science stuff

Find the three polarized filters that came with the kit. They're the lightly tinted pieces you can see through. Hold one up and look through it at various things. Does it make anything look different? Try rotating the filter and see if that does anything.

"Bear? What bear? I can't see a thing, Larry.
Let me borrow your shades."

Figure 4.1

Now hold two filters together so you're looking through both of them. Slowly rotate one of the filters while keeping the second one stationary (Figure 4.1). You should definitely see something happening now.

Arrange these two filters so no light gets through them. What do you think will happen if you add a third filter to these two? Go ahead and try it. Does rotating this third filter change anything? Now you're ready for a magic trick (yippee!). With the first two filters set up so no light gets through, slide the third filter *in between* the first two and slowly rotate it. How in the world can adding a filter actually allow light to pass through? Shouldn't more filters result in more light being blocked? Evidently not!

Yet another magic trick. Use two polarized filters and a sheet of plastic wrap to make a sandwich. The filters should be oriented so no light gets through, with the plastic wrap in between. Now stretch the plastic wrap as shown in Figure 4.2. Proof positive that stretching is good for you, because it makes you see the light. Okay, bad joke.

Figure 4.2

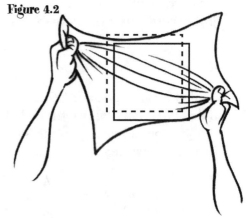

The science stuff

Hearken back to Chapter 2, where I explained how we can model light as changing electric and magnetic fields traveling through space as waves. Figure 2.14 (p. 30) is a drawing of that, and it gives the impression that the electric fields are always up and down and the magnetic fields are always side to side. That's not the case with most of the light you run into in everyday life. In fact, the electric and magnetic fields can be moving in any direction, as long as it's in the plane that's perpendicular to the direction of travel of the light waves (Figure 4.3).

Figure 4.3

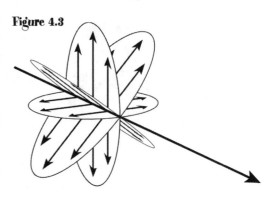

In general, any small bundle of light waves will have electric and magnetic fields that move in all of the directions of that plane. We call this kind of light

unpolarized light, and we can repre-sent it with a diagram like Figure 4.4.

To figure out what a polarized filter does to unpolarized light, I'm going to use an analogy of waves on a rope. Suppose you have a rope that goes through a narrow picket fence, as shown in Figure 4.5.[1]

Further suppose you want to send waves along that rope so they make it past

Figure 4.4

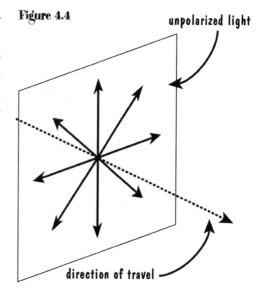

unpolarized light

direction of travel

Figure 4.5

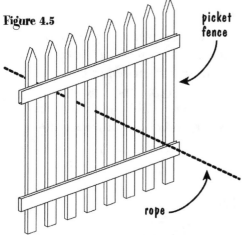

picket fence

rope

the picket fence. If those waves are in the same direction as the slots in the picket fence, you're in business. If they're perpendicular to the slots, the waves just won't make it through (Figure 4.6).

What about waves that are at a 45-degree angle to the slots in the fence? It might not be obvious, but what will make

Figure 4.6

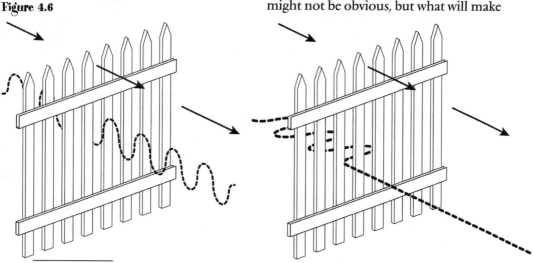

---

[1] For those Rocky and Bullwinkle fans out there, I'm reminded of the two guys sitting on a bench, talking, when something really strange happens in the cartoon. One turns to the other and says, "Now there's somethin' you don't see everyday, Chauncy—a rope going through a picket fence."

Figure 4.7

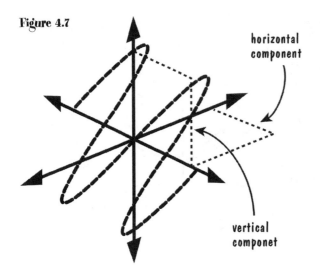

horizontal component

vertical componet

it through the fence is a *portion* of the waves. You can think of the waves at a 45-degree angle as having a vertical component and a horizontal component (Figure 4.7).

The vertical component gets through, but the horizontal component doesn't. The result is that part of the wave (the part that lines up with the slots) makes it through the fence.

Now let's suppose you are the fastest waves-on-a-rope maker in the West. You can send a bunch of waves along a rope, and change their direction really fast so it looks like you're simultaneously sending waves that move in every direction in the plane that's perpendicular to the direction of travel of the waves, as seen in Figure 4.8.

When you try and send this mess through the fence, the fence will "select out" all of the waves that move in the direction of the slots plus parts of the waves that are not completely perpendicular to the slots. The waves that are completely perpendicular to the slots won't make it through at all. On the other side of the fence, you end up with waves that are moving in only one direction—the direction of the slots (Figure 4.9).

Polarized filters do just about the same thing to light that goes through them. Unpolarized light has its electric fields vibrating in all directions in the plane that's perpendicular to the direction of travel of the waves. The filter "selects" out only those waves with entire electric fields, or components of electric fields, that vibrate in a particular direction. Exactly half of the unpo-

Figure 4.8

Figure 4.9

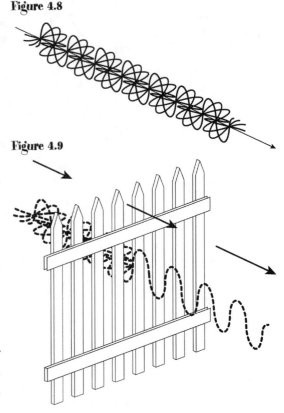

larized light makes it through the filter, and what does make it through has its electric field vibrating in only one direction (Figure 4.10). Any light with an electric field vibrating in only one direction is called **polarized light.**

How does a polarized filter perform this magic? Just about the same way that picket fences perform this magic on waves on a rope. Polarized filters are composed of long chain molecules that are lined up along a particular direction, much like the pickets in a picket fence. These molecules completely absorb light that has its electric fields lined up with the molecules and they just reradiate (basically, let pass) light that has its electric fields perpendicular to the molecules. This is like the picket fence absorbing waves that are lined up with the slots, so the analogy breaks down a bit, but the final result is the same (see Figure 4.11).

Let's now look at what happens when you try and send rope waves through two picket

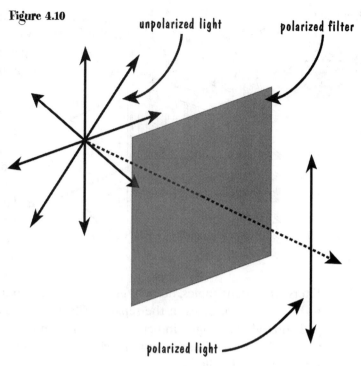

Figure 4.10

unpolarized light

polarized filter

polarized light

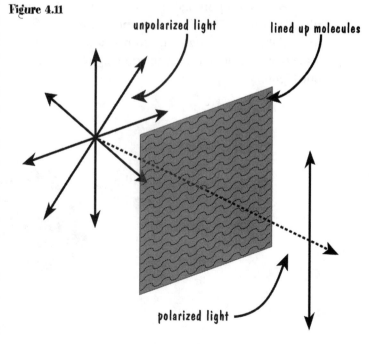

Figure 4.11

unpolarized light

lined up molecules

polarized light

Figure 4.12

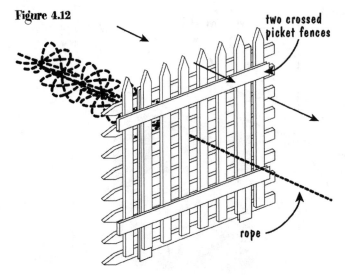

two crossed
picket fences

rope

fences. The trick is that these two fences have their slots lined up at right angles to each other (Figure 4.12).

Obviously no waves are going to make it through both fences. The first fence selects out waves that are traveling up and down, but those are precisely the waves that won't make it through the second fence. The same thing happens with two polarized filters. When they're set up so the chain molecules in the separate filters are at right angles, no light gets through. Of course, if the filters are set up so the chain molecules in the separate filters are exactly lined up, lots of light gets through. For angles in between, varying amounts of light get through both filters. That's why there's a gradual change from light to dark when you slowly rotate one of the filters.

Makes perfect sense, right? Well, what in the world is going on when you have two filters at right angles letting no light through and then slip a third in between, resulting in light getting through? To understand this, we look at two filters at a time. The first filter and the middle filter are not at right angles, so some light gets through this combination. The middle filter and the last filter also are not at right angles, so some light gets through that combination. Check out Figure 4.13.

Figure 4.13

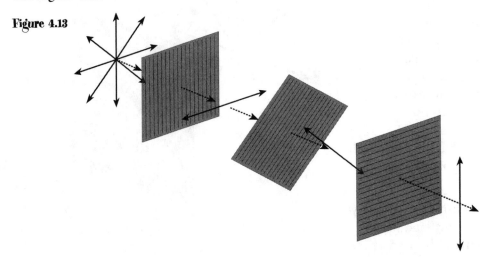

Finally, let's figure out what's going on with the plastic wrap sandwiched between the two filters that are at right angles (no light getting through). When you stretch the plastic wrap, all of a sudden light gets through. In other words, the plastic wrap starts acting like a polarized filter. The reason for that is that by stretching the plastic wrap, you actually *do* make it into a polarized filter. Plastic wrap is composed of long chain molecules, but they're not lined up like a picket fence. When you stretch the plastic, you line those molecules up, and you end up with a polarized filter.

More things to do before you read more science stuff

There's really only one thing to do in this section, but it is definitely worth doing. Put some clear corn syrup in a glass (half full is fine) and then tape one of the polarized filters to the side of the glass. Then set up a flashlight so it shines through the filter and then on through the corn syrup. Figure 4.14 explains it all.

Figure 4.14

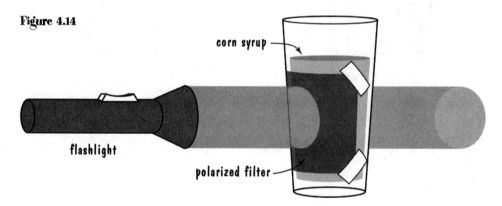

corn syrup

flashlight

polarized filter

Hold a second polarized filter in front of you as you look at the light emerging from the corn syrup. Rotate the filter and see all the pretty colors! Rotate the filter slowly and notice the progression of colors. Any special order in which they appear?

More science stuff

Because the light from the flashlight passes through a polarized filter, the light that goes through the corn syrup is polarized in a certain direction. Just as when light goes through any kind of medium, this polarized light doesn't just pass on through the corn syrup. It's absorbed and reradiated as it passes through. Sugar molecules, such as dextrose and fructose (of which corn syrup is made), *rotate* the direction of polarization of light in this absorption and reradiation process. And just as different frequencies of light refract different amounts in most mediums, different frequencies of light have their directions of polarization rotated different amounts when they travel through sugar molecules. So let's say red light rotates the amount shown in Figure 4.15, and blue light rotates the amount shown in Figure 4.16.

Figure 4.15
red light

Figure 4.16
blue light

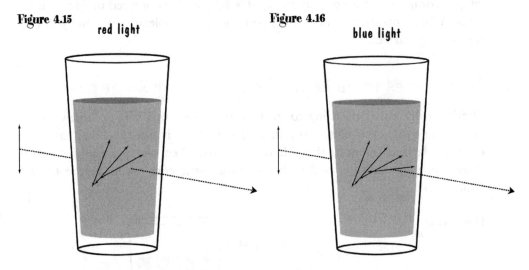

What happens when you look at this emerging light through a second polarized filter and slowly rotate that filter? You will see the red light at one angle and blue light at another. And of course you'll see all the other colors in between.

Chapter Summary

- Unpolarized light is light that has electric fields vibrating in all directions in a plane perpendicular to the direction the light travels.

- Polarized light is light that has electric fields vibrating in a single direction.

- Certain materials can create polarized light from unpolarized light, stop light with a given polarization direction from passing, or rotate the direction in which light is polarized.

Applications

1. Okay, what about those polarized sunglasses? What's special about them? Well, they're supposed to reduce glare and they do. Reflected light, as in light from the Sun hitting the car in front of you and shining in your eyes, tends to be polarized in a direction that's parallel to the surface from which

it's reflecting.[2] If you have sunglasses that are polarized perpendicular to that direction, those sunglasses will absorb much of the reflected light. Hence, they reduce glare.

2. Speaking of sunglasses, why is it that car windshields look all blotchy when you have polarized sunglasses on? This relates back to the plastic wrap. Windshields, and other glass, tend to have stress points, where the molecules of the glass are stretched to the point where they act like polarizing filters. By looking at that glass through another polarizing filter (the sunglasses), you see areas where the two filters do and don't line up.

3. Remember why the sky is blue? It has to do with how the tiny molecules in the upper atmosphere scatter sunlight. Turns out that during that scattering process, the emerging blue light tends to be polarized more in one direction than others. To see this, go out on a sunny day and look at the sky (with the Sun off to your left or right) through one of the polarized filters. Rotate the filter and see that the blue light coming at you is polarized.

4. Oh boy, another field trip to the local rock shop! Ask to see a sample of *calcite*. Hold the piece of calcite over some print and rotate it. You'll see a double image in certain orientations. That's because calcite has a different index of refraction (check Chapter 1 if you don't remember what an index of refraction is) for light that is polarized in different directions. Now, just as we can think of light that is polarized at a 45-degree angle as having a vertical and a horizontal component (see Figure 4.7), we can also represent unpolarized light as being a combination of vertically and horizontally polarized light. The calcite takes the unpolarized light coming off the print and splits it into two images because the different polarizations (vertical and horizontal components) refract different amounts.

---

[2] To be exact, the reflected light is *elliptically polarized*, but that whole idea would take another page to explain, and you probably don't care anyway!

When Light Waves Collide

I told you way back in Chapter 1 that light doesn't always travel in straight lines. It can bend around corners, just like sound. When it does change direction like this, you end up with light waves that originated from different places coming together at one spot. This can lead to some really cool effects and pretty colors. You saw those colors when you looked through the diffraction grating that came with the book. You get to find out how that thing works in this chapter.

5 Chapter

Things to do before you read the science stuff

What better way to start learning more about light than by messing around with sound? That might seem silly, but because we can model both light and sound as waves, they behave very much alike. Plus, you'd need a laser to do with light what you're about to do with sound, and I'm betting most of you don't have a laser in the attic. If you do happen to have a laser, I'll tell you later how to use it to do the following demonstration.

So on to what you have to do. Set up your home sound system or a boom box so two of the speakers are right next to each other and facing the same direction (you do need two speakers for this, so a regular radio won't work). Place the speakers so you can be about 3 meters away from them with your ears at the level of the speakers. You'll have to get down on hands and knees if the speakers are on the floor (Figure 5.1).

Figure 5.1

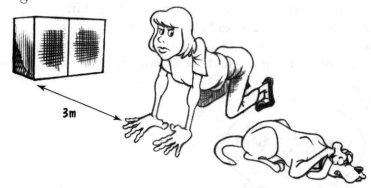

3m

Do whatever you must to pick up AM radio signals. If you have a mono/stereo button on your sound system, set it for mono. Now tune the receiver so you're in between stations and picking up that really annoying *weeeeooooo* sort of high-pitched hum that you would normally try to avoid. This annoying hum is easier to find with a dial tuner than with a push-button digital tuner. If all you have is the latter, just do the best you can to find a constant pitch hum with as little static, talking, or music as possible.

With one ear facing the speakers, move your head *slowly* back and forth in the direction shown in Figure 5.2. Concentrate on the annoying hum as you do this and notice any change in

Figure 5.2

volume. Is there also an overall pattern to the changes in volume? Are you getting coded messages from outer space?

Time for some serious science experimentation. Scrounge around the kids' rooms for some bubble blowing solution, go outside on a sunny day, and blow some bubbles. Watch the bubbles carefully as they float around. In addition to seeing reflections in the bubbles (which you could explain using ray diagrams, right?), you can also see lots of swirling colors. What's causing those? While you're at it, think about the last time you saw a thin film of oil on water (the street after a rain is a good place to see this—the oil is from the cars and the water is from, um, the sky). What causes the colors you see in this oil film?

The science stuff

Suppose you and a friend hold opposite ends of a rope and send wave pulses toward the middle of the rope. When those pulses meet, they're each telling the rope to do something (go up, go down, or stay still). Being an innocent by-stander in this process, the rope does what both pulses tell it to do. If each pulse says "go up," then the rope rises twice as high as it would with just one pulse. If each pulse says, "go down," then the rope goes down twice as much. If one pulse says to go up and the other says to go down, those instructions cancel each other, and the rope does nothing (Figure 5.3).

Light waves and sound waves do the same kind of thing. If waves from two separate sources hit a spot "in phase," meaning up-and-down motions are in

Figure 5.3

twice as high   pulses cancel out

Figure 5.4

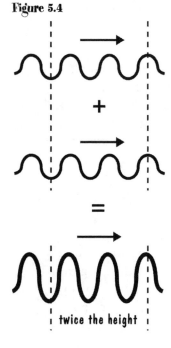

twice the height

Figure 5.5

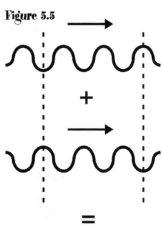

waves cancel and
you get nothing

sync, then the total effect at that spot is twice what it would normally be (Figure 5.4).

If the two sources are "out of phase," meaning their up-and-down motions are totally out of sync, then the two waves cancel each other and you get nothing (Figure 5.5).

This process of completely adding, completely canceling, or something in between, is known as **interference.** When two or more waves combine to produce a greater result than the individual waves, that's called **constructive interference,** and when two or more waves combine to produce a lesser result (they cancel one another) than the individual waves, that's called **destructive interference.**

Let's apply this idea to the sound waves coming from the two speakers. Figure 5.6 shows that the waves coming from each speaker usually travel different distances in getting to a given place.

In traveling different distances, the two sets of waves can get "out of step" with each other. We can think of this process as one wave shifting with respect to the other. If the total amount of shift is a wavelength, or multiples of a wavelength, the two sets of waves will still be in sync (in phase), and they'll interfere constructively. This gives you a loud spot. If the total amount of shift is a half a wavelength, or odd multiples of half a wavelength, the two sets of waves will

Figure 5.6

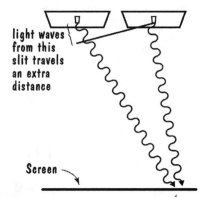

waves from this speaker travel an extra distance

light waves from this slit travels an extra distance

Screen

Just as with speakers, light reaching this point from one slit has traveled farther than light from the other slit.

be totally out of sync (out of phase), and they'll interfere destructively. This gives you a quiet spot (Figure 5.7).

Figure 5.7

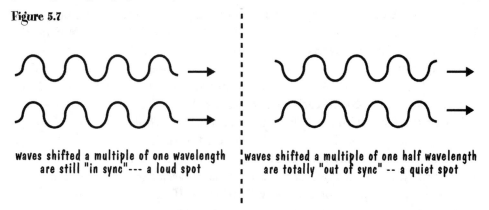

waves shifted a multiple of one wavelength are still "in sync"--- a loud spot

waves shifted a multiple of one half wavelength are totally "out of sync" -- a quiet spot

Overall, you end up with a pattern of loud-soft-loud-soft-loud-soft as you move around the speakers, as shown in Figure 5.8. This is due to the sound waves from the separate speakers getting in and out of phase because they travel different distances to get to you.

As I said, light does the same thing. However, setting up this demonstration with light is trickier, mainly because light has such a short wavelength. The way you do it is to shine a laser at two very tiny, closely spaced slits. These two slits act like two separate sources of light (like the two speakers), and they will produce a series of light and dark spots on a screen held in front of the slits (Figure 5.9).

Figure 5.8

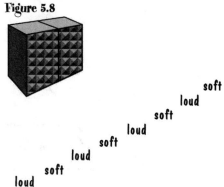

soft
loud
soft
loud
soft
loud
soft
loud
soft
loud

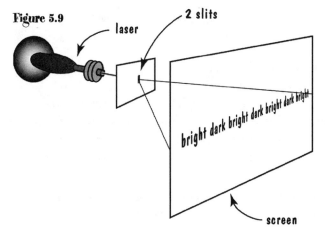

Figure 5.9

laser

2 slits

bright dark bright dark bright dark bright

screen

I could take this a bit further and develop a mathematical relationship that will tell exactly where the light and dark spots will be (at what angle from the two slits) for a given wavelength of incoming light and a given separation of the slits. If I did that, though, then I'd be following the usual high school and college textbook route, and this isn't a textbook! Besides, a whole bunch of math and geometry right now might make you put down this book and never pick it up again.

Let's move on to oil films and soap bubbles. Exactly the same kind of process is going on with both of them, so I'll only explain the oil film. When light hits a thin oil film, it reflects from the front surface and also the back surface.[1] Now suppose you have light of a single wavelength (one color) hitting this film. Figure 5.10 shows what happens to this light when it hits the film at two different angles. Notice that in each case, the light that reflects off the back of the film travels farther than the light that reflects off the front of the film. This sets up the possibility that the two sets of reflected waves could shift in relation to each other, and possibly get out of phase. If the extra distance traveled causes those two waves to get out of sync by a half wavelength, they will interfere destructively, and you won't see any light at all. If the extra distance traveled causes the waves to be back in phase when they emerge, you'll see a bright spot.

Figure 5.10

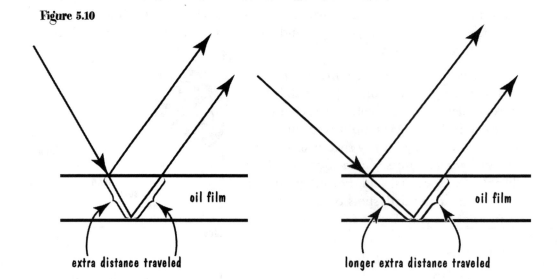

To be more realistic, consider what will happen when white light, containing all colors, hits our oil film. We still have the same situation, with one crucial difference. Because the different colors of light have different wavelengths, the extra distance traveled will get them in or out of phase by different amounts. So if the angle is just right to cause red light to interfere destructively, other wavelengths of light *won't* interfere destructively. The result is that

---

[1] This is just like the situation that makes double pane windows create double images, only on a much smaller scale. I discussed that in the Applications section of Chapter 1.

you remove red from the white light and you see a greenish blue color. Viewing this oil film from different angles will result in colors other than red interfering destructively, and you'll see different colors. Put it all together and you get a rainbow of colors (Figure 5.11).

Soap bubbles work just about the same, with the soap film replacing the oil film in the explanation. In both instances, different thicknesses of the films also figure into what colors you see where, but I'll leave that analysis as a homework assignment!

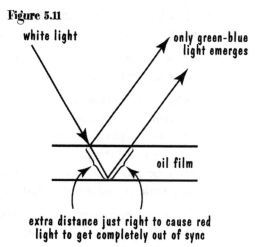

Figure 5.11

white light

only green-blue light emerges

oil film

extra distance just right to cause red light to get completely out of sync

More things to do before you read more science stuff

Set up your lamp with the long, tube-shaped bulb that I asked you to get in Chapter 3. You didn't really have to go out and buy this bulb in Chapter 3 but now you have to. So there. Get two index cards, hold them right in front of your face, and bring them together so you are looking at the bulb through a really narrow slit (Figure 5.12).

Experiment with the size of the slit until you see something really interesting, such as a whole bunch of vertical lines of dark and light. What happens to the spacing between these lines as you change the width of the slit?

To get an even better view of those vertical lines, get a fork from the kitchen. Hold it as shown in Figure 5.13 and *slowly* rotate it so when you look through the tines of the fork, you are essentially looking through slits of different widths.

Figure 5.12

2 index cards

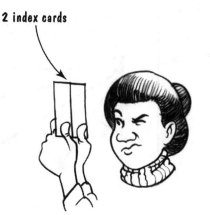

Figure 5.13

With a little care, you can rotate the fork slowly enough that you see a very gradual change in the pattern of lines.

Notice any colors in the pattern? You should. How in the world can a fork create rainbows? I thought you needed a prism for that!

Get your Rainbow Peephole (a diffraction grating) and look at the bulb through this. There are rainbows all over the place, but concentrate on the pattern of rainbows that stretch out directly to the right and left. See any similarity between this pattern and the pattern of lines created with the fork? This is a tough comparison, because the fork patterns are really close together, while the diffraction grating patterns are really spread out.

Finally, tape an empty toilet paper tube to the end of a flashlight and then poke a pinhole in a sheet of construction paper. Set all of this up as in Figure 5.14, so the light from the flashlight goes through the pinhole and shines onto a wall.

Take a close look at the pattern created on the wall. Any similarity between this pattern and what you get with a narrow slit?

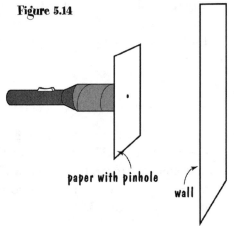

Figure 5.14

paper with pinhole

wall

More science stuff

In what follows, I'm going to talk about what made those patterns you observed as light went through a narrow slit. The explanation is going to involve the light spreading out as it travels through the slit, as in Figure 5.15.[2]

Why does the light spread out, though? Why doesn't the light just travel straight on

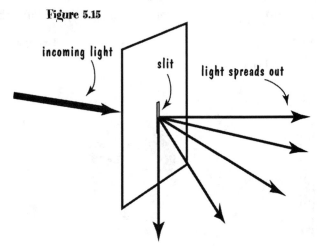

Figure 5.15

incoming light

slit

light spreads out

[2] Notice that Figure 5.15 only shows the light spreading out horizontally and not vertically. For reasons I won't go into here, light spreads out significantly only when the size of the opening is close to the wavelength of the incoming light. Because we've arranged things so the vertical dimension of the slit is *much* larger than a wavelength of light, there's very little spreading in that direction.

through, as in Figure 5.16? After all, that's what you'd expect if light traveled in straight lines.

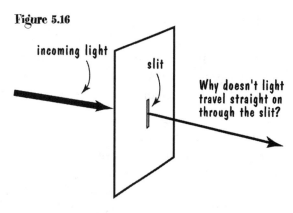

Figure 5.16

incoming light

slit

Why doesn't light travel straight on through the slit?

The key to what's going on here lies in the edges of the narrow slit. Remember that light doesn't just pass by or through things but rather is always being absorbed and reradiated. The light at the edge of the slit is absorbed by whatever material the slit is made of and then reradiated. It's as if the light at that point is a whole new source of light (which it is!). In fact, it's accurate to picture the light emerging from the slit as coming from many, many point sources of light.

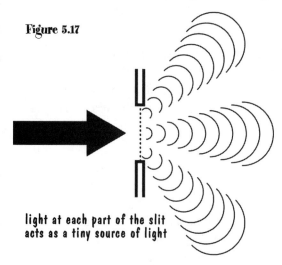

Figure 5.17

light at each part of the slit acts as a tiny source of light

Okay, so the light spreads out when it passes through the slit (Figure 5.17). To see what this means in terms of creating lots of dark and light lines, consider what happens when light from one side of the slit meets up with light from the other side of the slit at a point on a distant screen.

As Figure 5.18 shows, waves from these two sources of light travel different distances to get to the point on the screen. That means they can get out of sync, and

either constructively or destructively interfere with each other. In other words, we have the same situation as we had with two point sources of light interfering with each other. That means we're going to get a pattern of light and dark regions. Well, the situation isn't exactly like two point sources. We have *lots* of point sources (infinitely many, in fact)! I won't go into the math, because it involves calculus, but the overall result of the interference of all

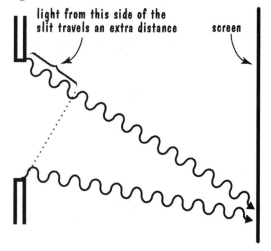

Figure 5.18

light from this side of the slit travels an extra distance

screen

these infinitely small sources of light is a pattern that's a lot like what you get from two point sources. What you have to do is add up all the shifts in wavelength from the infinite number of point sources of light and see what you get in terms of constructive or destructive interference. Sounds complicated but it's not if you understand the basics of calculus[3].

When you get a pattern of light and dark lines by sending light through a single slit, it's called **diffraction.** I'm sure there's a historical reason for making a distinction between interference and diffraction, but you should know that *they are exactly the same thing.* You have different sources of light interfering constructively and destructively to produce various patterns. When you have two or three or five sources of light, physicists call it interference. When you have a whole bunch of sources of light, physicists call it diffraction. So if you have to take a physics test before passing through the Pearly Gates, and one of the questions is "What's the difference between interference and diffraction?" the correct answer is "nothing." You might still get it marked wrong, but at least you'll have the satisfaction of knowing you're right.

Before getting to the colors in the patterns, we can take care of the pinhole image without much trouble. Because the pinhole is circular, it produces a pattern of light and dark lines that is circular. It's the same old diffraction, but in two dimensions instead of one. In this case, there is spreading in all directions because the diameter of the pinhole is relatively close to the wavelength of the incoming light (see Footnote 2, page 76).

Figure 5.19

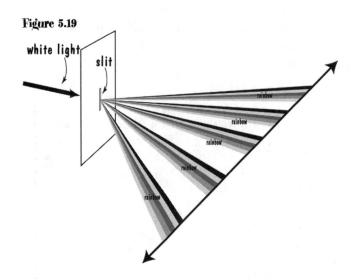

white light

slit

rainbow
rainbow
rainbow
rainbow
rainbow

Okay, what about those colors? Well, it's a lot like the interference that happens with an oil or soap film. Remember that each color of light has a different wavelength. For a given path difference, some colors (wavelengths) will interfere constructively and some will interfere destructively. So as you move along the path shown in Figure 5.19, you will encounter spots where different colors are bright, leading to those nice little rainbows.

---

[3] Calculus, and math in general, is another one of those subjects that sends people running for cover. Just like science, though, it really isn't that difficult to understand conceptually. It just *looks* intimidating.

And now the moment you've been waiting for. I'm going to explain how your diffraction grating works. A diffraction grating is basically plastic or glass with lots of narrowly spaced lines etched in it. When light hits a diffraction grating, it's as if the light is going through thousands of narrow slits. Light waves from all these slits interfere with one another, creating a series of bright and dark regions.

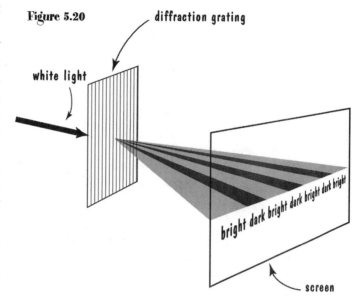

Figure 5.20

diffraction grating

white light

bright dark bright dark bright dark bright

screen

Each of these bright and dark regions is separated into different colors, for exactly the reasons described for a single slit. So you will notice a series of rainbows spreading out from the center, each a bit fainter than the one before it. Clearly, though, your Rainbow Peephole doesn't exactly correspond to Figure 5.20. That's because the Rainbow Peephole is really two diffraction gratings placed at right angles. This arrangement leads to patterns that scatter off along four different lines.

Chapter Summary

- When separate light waves arrive at a given spot, those waves can add constructively (add to each other to create a larger wave), add destructively (cancel each other), or produce a result somewhere in between those two extremes. All kinds of wave addition are known as *interference*.

- Interference using a relatively small number of sources of light is simply termed *interference*. Interference using a large number of sources of light is usually termed *diffraction*.

- Interference and diffraction cause white light to separate into its component colors, thus having an effect similar to that of sending light through a prism.

5 Chapter

Applications

1. Does anything ever cast a clean, sharp shadow? If light travels in straight lines, that's what you'd expect. That's not what happens, though. The reason is that light doesn't behave like a simple ray model and travel in straight lines. Because light interacts with the edge of the object creating the shadow, there is a bit of diffraction taking place, and the edge of the shadow is a bit fuzzy. If you have a carefully controlled shadow setup, you can look closely and see that the fuzzy area of the shadow is actually composed of a series of light and dark lines, as shown in Figure 5.21. Hmmmmm. Wonder what causes those?

Figure 5.21

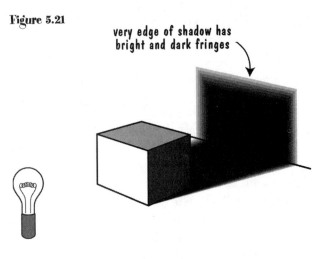

very edge of shadow has bright and dark fringes

2. Ever wonder why your CD collection produces rainbows when light shines on the CDs? It's basically an interference effect. A CD is etched in a certain way so that a laser reflecting off of it reproduces the pattern contained in the music. The etches in the CD are close together, much like a diffraction grating. When light reflects off these etches, it's just as if the light is coming from many tiny light sources. This leads to the same kind of pattern (rainbows!) you get with a diffraction grating. In fact, you would call a CD a *reflection* grating.

3. When there's a full moon and a light cloud cover, you will sometimes see colored rings around the moon. Why? Interference as the moonlight passes through the tiny water droplets that compose clouds.

4. Holograms are special pictures that produce a realistic 3-D effect. When you move your head, you can actually see different sides of the object in a hologram. Try that with a regular picture! The creation of holograms relies on the interference of light that reflects off different parts of an object. For example, suppose we're taking a picture of your face. Light that travels from a light source, to your nose, and then to a camera, travels a different distance than light that travels from the source, to your cheek, and then to a camera. These different distances mean that the two different reflected light waves are probably out of sync when they hit the camera. Exactly how much they're

out of sync is a clue to how far your cheek is from your nose. In order to make holograms, you have to have a very special setup that preserves the "phase relationship" between different light waves. I won't go into that, but you should know that the basic principle of holograms is just plain ol' interference of light waves.

5. In the desert of New Mexico, there's a huge collection of radio telescopes known as the Very Large Array. Put that name into an Internet search engine for a picture of the array. This large grid of telescopes works a lot like a diffraction grating in reverse. It's "reverse" because instead of sending out electromagnetic waves, this collection receives electromagnetic waves. By using the interference effect of the radio waves that hit all the different telescopes, it's possible for this array to focus in on signals coming from a very tiny part of the sky. They simply set up the array so that all signals except the ones in that tiny part of the sky interfere destructively, and the ones from that part of the sky interfere constructively.

SCI
LINKS.
THE WORLD'S A CLICK AWAY

Topic: interference

Go to: *www.scilinks.org*

Code: SFL09

Topic: diffraction

Go to: *www.scilinks.org*

Code: SFL10

All About Eyeballs

This chapter is, as the title indicates, all about eyeballs and how they work. We'll use just about everything we've learned so far, plus one or two new things, including how to draw 3-D pictures.

Things to do before you read the science stuff

I'm going to ask you to do a number of little projects, one right after the other. They all have to do with how your eyes work, but you might not see how until I tie them all together in the next section. In the meantime, get started!

"The doctor told me to keep an eye on things.
But, he didn't say which one."

Close your eyes and very gently touch the top part of your eyeball (through the eyelid) where the eyeball meets the bone just above your eye. Push gently with your finger. You should "see" an image at the bottom of your eye. Repeat this at the bottom of your eyeball and you'll 'see" an image at the top of your eye. Odd, no?

Grab a flashlight and head to the bathroom mirror. Look closely at your eyes in the mirror. As you do this, shine the flashlight toward one of your eyes. Then repeatedly turn the flashlight on and off. What happens to your eyes as you do this?

Take a red and a blue object (the red and blue filters are fine) into a dimly lit room. A closet with the door just barely open should work. Make sure you are able to see everything around you, just not very well. Look at the red and blue objects in this dimly lit room. Which do you see better? Now take them out into a bright room. Which one seems brighter now?

You need a friend for this next part. Gather together several different colors of paper and give them to the friend. Sit and stare straight ahead while your friend slowly brings one color of paper from behind your head to where you can just see the paper out of your peripheral (side) vision. *Don't* move your eyes to look at it!

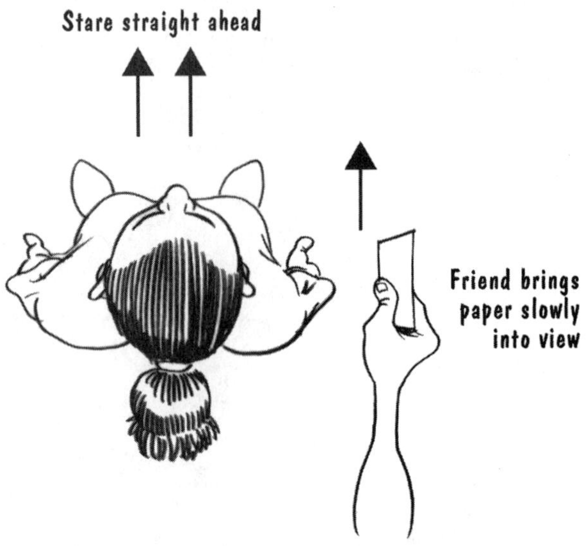

Stop your friend as soon as you can see the paper. Try to identify the color of the paper. Do this a bunch of times with different colored paper and see how good you are at identifying colors with your peripheral vision (Figure 6.1).

Figure 6.1

Stare straight ahead

Friend brings paper slowly into view

Get a red object and a sheet of white paper (no lines). Any old red object will do, as long as it's not bigger than the sheet of paper. Put the red object on the paper and then stare at the object for at least 30 seconds. If you can handle a minute, that's even better. Now remove the red object and stare for a while at the white paper. After a while, an image of the object should appear. What color is it? Repeat this using a green object and an orange object.

Figure 6.2 shows two *xs*. Hold this book about 30 centimeters (a foot) from your face, cover your left eye, and stare at the *x* on the left with your right eye.

Figure 6.2

Move the book slowly toward and away from you. At one point, the *x* on the right should disappear. Repeat this, covering your right eye and staring at the *x* on the right with your left eye.

The science stuff

Figure 6.3

Figure 6.3 shows a diagram of what a cross section of your eye looks like.

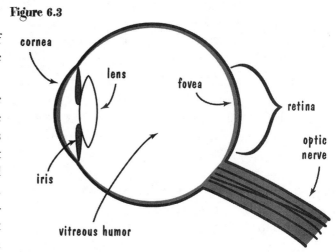

The *cornea* and the *lens* combine to focus light on the back of the eye, on what is known as the *retina*. This is just the same kind of thing any old convex lens would do to light, meaning that it creates an up-side-down image on the back of your eye. Also, something in the bottom of your field of view shows up as an image on the top part of the back of your eye (Figure 6.4).

Figure 6.4

When you gen-tly push on the top of your eye, you "see" something in the bottom of your field of view. This is because you have stimulated the *top* of

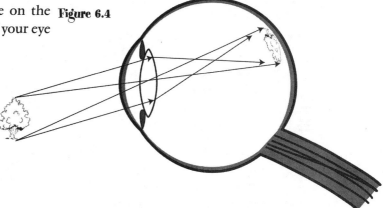

the back of your eye, and your brain therefore thinks it's seeing something down low. So obviously, your brain seems to know that whatever image hits the back of the eye is upside down!

Another cool thing about the lens is that your eye has muscles that can actually change the shape of the lens. This changes the focal length of the lens

Topic: the eye

Go to: *www.sciLINKS.org*

Code: SFL11

and helps you focus on objects that are different distances from you.

When you shone a flashlight in one of your eyes, you saw your *iris* expand and contract. That's because little muscles in your eye react to the amount of light coming in and adjust the opening accordingly. Too much light makes it really difficult to see things, so when you shine light in your eyes, the opening gets smaller. When you go to the optometrist and get your eyes dilated, they paralyze these tiny muscles in the eye so your iris stays wide open. Unfortunately, the muscles that control the focusing power of the lens also get paralyzed. You end up with a double whammy— too much light getting in and no ability to focus—that makes it really difficult to drive home!

Figure 6.3 shows something called the *fovea* in the center of the retina on the back of your eye. The fovea contains lots of little light receptors called *cones*. Surrounding the fovea are other kinds of light receptors called *rods*. Rods and cones both react when light waves hit them but they react in different ways. First, rods are more active in dim light and cones are more active in bright light. Rods are also more sensitive to the blue end of the spectrum, while cones are more sensitive to the red end of the spectrum This explains what happened when you looked at red and blue objects in a dimly lit room and then in a bright room. In the dimly lit room, the rods take over and you are able to see the blue object better. The red object might even appear black. In the bright room, the cones are the primary receptors, and you see both objects equally well, or possibly the red one seems a bit brighter than the blue one.

Now even though the rods do detect color, they don't do it very well. And notice that because the rods are on the edge of the fovea, they are the receptors we use in peripheral vision.[1] So when you use your peripheral vision, you can't make out colors very well. Interestingly, though, your peripheral vision can detect *motion* quite well, so even if you don't know whether it's black or brown, you can tell that some kind of bear is sneaking up on you!

The exact mechanism of how rods and cones perceive color isn't all that well understood, but we do know that there are pigments (the primary one is called *visual purple*) that respond differently to different frequencies of light. We also know that you can "overload" your eye's response to certain frequencies. When you stared at the red object and then at a blank sheet of paper, you saw a green image of the object. That's because your eyes became desensitized to the fre-

---

[1] Remember how lenses form images. An image in your peripheral vision will form on the edge of the retina, where the rods are, rather than the center, where the cones are.

quencies of red light, effectively removing that color from your detection system for a while. Of course, the ability to overload your eye receptors isn't always a bad thing, as I'll explain in the Applications section.

Finally, what's going on with the blind spot in your eye? How is it possible to make one of the x's on the page disappear? Well, there's one spot on your eye where there are no rods or cones. It's the place where the nerves that lead from the rods and cones exit the eyeball on their way to the brain, and they are collectively known as the *optic nerve*. The trick with the disappearing x just amounts to arranging things so the image of the x falls right on the optic nerve, exactly where you don't have any receptors to detect the image.

More things to do before you read more science stuff

I promised 3-D pictures, and that's what you'll get. Get a clean white sheet of paper (no lines), a red pencil, a blue pencil, and the red and blue filters. Start by drawing a blue square on the sheet of paper. Don't press hard in this or any other step of what I'm going to have you draw. Using the red pencil (don't press hard!), draw an identical square that is shifted just slightly to the left of the blue square (Figure 6.5). The red and blue lines should overlap on the top and bottom. The more you can make these two squares the exact same size and shape, the better.

Figure 6.5

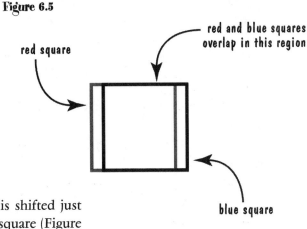

red square

red and blue squares overlap in this region

blue square

Now draw another blue square that slightly overlaps the first two squares (Figure 6.6).

Figure 6.6

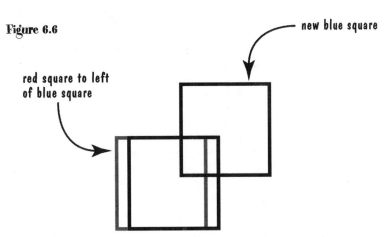

red square to left of blue square

new blue square

Overlap the new blue square exactly with the red pencil (Figure 6.7).

Figure 6.7

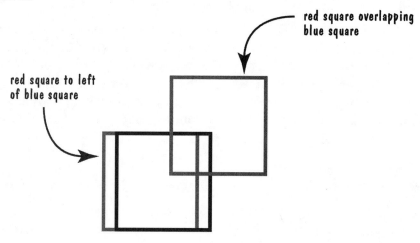

red square overlapping
blue square

red square to left
of blue square

Overlap this square with a third blue square (Figure 6.8).

Figure 6.8

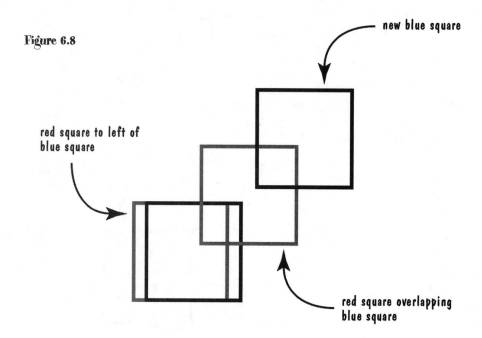

new blue square

red square to left of
blue square

red square overlapping
blue square

Now draw a red square identical to this last blue square, but shifted slightly to the *right* (Figure 6.9).

Figure 6.9

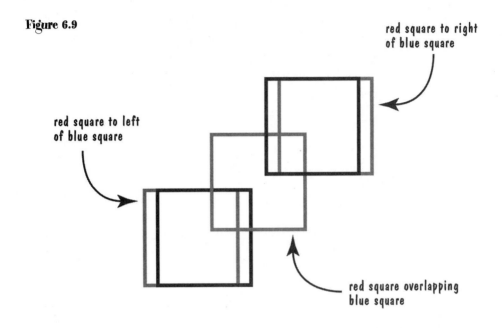

red square to right
of blue square

red square to left
of blue square

red square overlapping
blue square

Okay, time for the 3-D effect. Place the blue filter over your right eye and the red filter over the left eye, and look at your squares in bright light. You should see them as being different distances from you. The longer you stare at them, the better the effect becomes. Just for kicks, place the red filter over your right eye and the blue filter over your left eye. See any difference?

If you just came for the 3-D drawings and don't care what caused them, skip the rest of this section. If you want to understand what's going on, then you really better do the next couple of things.

Close one eye and walk around trying to pick up various objects. Easy or difficult compared to using two eyes?

Hold your finger right in front of your eyes and look at it first with one eye closed and then with the other eye closed. Notice the apparent shift in position of your finger as you do this. Now repeat with your finger at arm's length from your eyes. How does the amount of shift compare with when your finger was close to your eyes? Repeat this with all sorts of nearby and faraway objects. See a correlation between how far away something is and how much shift there is between the left and right eye images? See how people stare at you if you go around doing this in public?

More science stuff

We use a number of cues to determine how far away something is, but one of the primary ones is through the different images our two eyes see. Somehow our brain compares the image from each eye, determines the amount of shift in the images, and assigns a distance based on that shift. If the difference in shift is a lot, the object is close by. If the difference in shift is very little, the object is far away. Check out Figure 6.10.

Figure 6.10

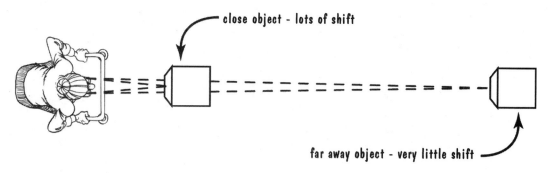

close object - lots of shift

far away object - very little shift

This explains why it's a little tricky picking up objects when you have one eye closed. There's no comparison to go by, and it's difficult to tell how far away the object is. This also explains the 3-D squares you drew. Basically, you are creating an artificial amount of shift to fool your eyes into seeing depth where there is none. Here's how it works. When you have a blue filter over your right eye and a red filter over your left eye, your right eye sees only the red lines and your left eye sees only the blue lines. Check back to Chapter 2, Application 1, for an explanation of that.

When the blue and red squares overlap exactly, there's just the normal shift between your left and right eye images for something that's on that piece of paper. You see one square. When the blue square is shifted to the right relative to the red square, your left eye sees a square that's shifted more than normal to the right and your right eye sees a square that's shifted more than normal to the left. Your brain assumes your left and right eyes are looking at a single square. Because there's lots of shift between the two images, your brain decides this square is closer to you than the sheet of paper (see Figure 6.11).

When the blue square is shifted to the left relative to the red square, your left eye sees a square that's shifted *less* than normal to the right and your right

Figure 6.11

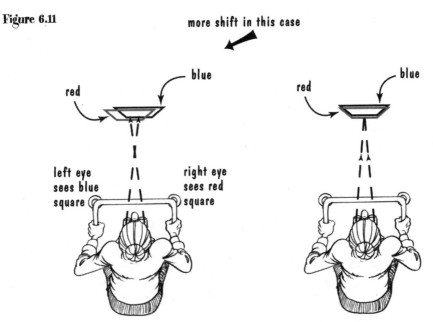

more shift in this case

blue

red

blue

red

left eye
sees blue
square

right eye
sees red
square

eye sees a square that's shifted *less* than normal to the left. Again your brain assumes your left and right eyes are looking at a single square. Because there's very little shift between the two images, your brain decides this square is farther away than the sheet of paper (Figure 6.12).

If you've been to a 3-D movie lately, chances are you looked at the screen not with red and blue glasses, but what seem like an ordinary pair of sun-

Figure 6.12

less shift in this case

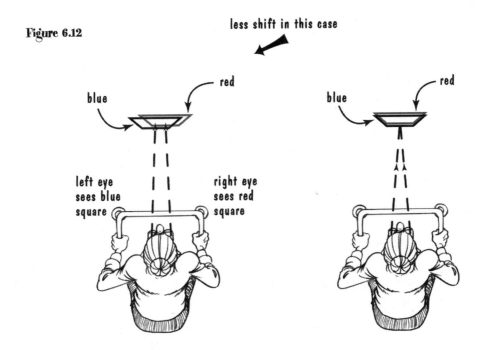

blue

red

blue

red

left eye
sees blue
square

right eye
sees red
square

glasses. Well, those aren't ordinary sunglasses. They're polarized sunglasses, with one lens polarized in one direction and the other lens polarized in the other direction. The movie itself is shown with two projectors. The two projectors are in sync, but they project images that are polarized in different directions. In this way, your right eye sees one set of images and your left eye sees another set of images. By creating artificial shifts in these images, the polarization creates a 3-D effect. So it's exactly the same process as using blue and red filters.

Chapter Summary

- The combination of cornea and lens in the eye act as a convex lens to focus images on the back part of the eyeball.

- The retina on the back of the eyeball contains light sensitive *rods* and *cones* that detect images and send appropriate information about the images to the brain.

- Rods and cones are sensitive to different frequency ranges and different strengths of light.

- We perceive distance, in part, by comparing the shift in an object's apparent position when viewed through the left and right eyes.

- We can create 3-D drawings and movies by causing the left and right eyes to see separate images and using those separate images to alter the amount of shift the brain perceives between the left and right eye images.

Figure 6.13

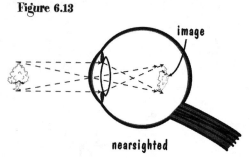

nearsighted

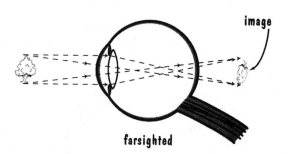

farsighted

Applications

1. When you're nearsighted, your lens and cornea combination focus light more strongly than necessary, creating an image in front of your retina.

   When you're farsighted, your lens and cornea combination focus light less strongly than necessary, creating an image behind your retina (Figure 6.13).

   To correct this, you use either a diverging lens (for nearsightedness) or a converging lens (for farsightedness) to get the image where it's supposed to be (Figure 6.14).

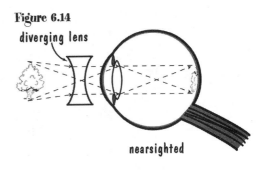

Figure 6.14
diverging lens

nearsighted

Of course, there's an easier way. Just change the shape of the cornea so it focuses light where it's supposed to. That's what LASIK surgery is all about.

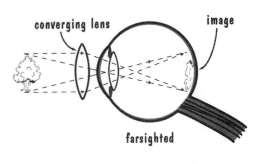

converging lens   image

farsighted

2. Ever wonder why you can't see very well under water? Well, in order for your eyes to focus properly, incoming light has to refract when it goes through the combination of cornea and lens. This refraction depends on the fact that the light is coming from air, with a low index of refraction, to the cornea, with a high index of refraction. Underwater, however, the incoming light goes from water to your cornea instead of from air to your cornea. Water has an index of refraction similar to that of your cornea, so the light doesn't refract very much. This means images don't focus where they're supposed to.

3. I told you that the fact you can overload your rods and cones is not all bad. That overloading leads to *persistence of vision*—the fact that you can see images for a short time after the original object is no longer there. Movie projectors present a whole bunch of still pictures at a rapid rate. This rate is fast enough that a new still picture appears before the image from the one before it fades. The result is that you see continuous motion rather than a series of still pictures.

Televisions and computer monitors use this same technique. Electron guns (!) sweep across the screen rapidly, creating the images you see. Before the image from the top of the screen can fade, the electron guns are back for a return trip that refreshes the image. Some computer monitors cheat on this effect. They don't refresh the entire screen each trip, but rather do only half the screen in each trip. This is called interlacing and results in a slight flickering of the screen image. If you don't want that flickering, make sure you buy a "noninterlacing" monitor.

4. Ever see little "floaters" in your field of vision? They're pretty easy to see if you go outside and stare at the sky (not directly at the Sun!). These little floaters go across your field of vision slowly, and move a bit if you blink.

Figure 6.15

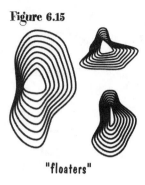

"floaters"

Watch them closely and you'll notice little rings around them.

Floaters are actually tiny particles that are in the vitreous humor on the inside of your eye. When light passes by them, they cause the light to diffract, creating the familiar pattern of light and dark lines (refer to Chapter 5). So basically, you're looking inside your eyeball when you see these little guys!

SCI LINKS.
THE WORLD'S A CLICK AWAY

Topic: LASIK

Go to: *www.scilinks.org*

Code: SFL12

Fire the Photon Torpe-does, Mr. Sulu!

Yeah, what about those photon torpedoes? Aren't photons supposed to be little light particles? Yes, they are, and they constitute the third model for what light is. Much of the photon stuff is beyond the scope of this book, but I can give you at least some idea of what photons are and maybe also some idea of what those electrons are actually doing when they emit visible light.

Things to do before you read the science stuff

This is the easiest "things to do" section in the whole book. All you have to do is make a list of all the things you can think of that produce light. Make sure you

only include things that produce their own light rather than reflect light from somewhere else. For example, the Sun produces its own light, but the Moon doesn't. We only see the Moon because of reflected sunlight. Glow-in-the-dark things should be included because, even though you have to charge them up by exposing them to another source of light, they produce their own light after that.

When you're done with your list, think of what all these things have in common, if anything. Well yeah, duh, they all produce light, but is there anything else they have in common?

The science stuff

Figure 7.1

"It's lonely at the bottom."

The current view of atoms is that the electrons in the atoms have a bunch of "energy levels" at which they can hang out. Some of those energy levels are occupied and some aren't. It's a bit like Figure 7.1, with each place higher up on the cliff corresponding to a higher energy level. There are all sorts of rules for how many electrons can be at each energy level and whether or not electrons are allowed to jump from one energy level to another.

There's a tendency for all atoms to have their electrons in the lowest energy condition possible. That means that if there's an opening in one of the lower energy levels, and the jump is allowed, an electron from a higher energy level will jump down to the lower energy level. As the electron jumps, it emits an electromagnetic wave. If the frequency of the emitted wave is in the visible range, then the electron has emitted light (Figure 7.2).

So, it's as simple as that. When an electron jumps from a higher energy level to a lower energy level, we

Figure 7.2

We have an opening for one...'light emitting' section...

light

get light. Of course, we don't have a very good picture of what the electrons are actually, physically doing. We know what they aren't doing, though. They're not jumping from shelf to shelf on a cliff, they're not buzzing around in circles, and they're not jiggling up and down.[1] For our purposes, though, "jumping from shelf to shelf" is a good enough analogy.

Now we know how to make an atom emit light. We cause its electrons to jump up to higher energy levels, leaving lower ones vacant. Then electrons jump down to these vacant levels, and emit light when they do. The way you cause electrons to jump to higher energy levels is to add energy to the atoms.[2] In a lightbulb, you run an electrical current through the filament. This *excites* the atoms (yes, that's the actual terminology scientists use—and you thought science wasn't sexy!), sending lots of electrons to higher energy states. When those electrons jump back down to lower levels they give us light.

Other sources of light use different kinds of energy to make them emit light. The Sun uses nuclear reactions. A match uses a chemical reaction known as *oxidation* to produce light. Glow sticks also use a chemical reaction. You have to snap a glow stick to get it to glow. When you snap it, two different chemicals inside the stick mix together. In the mixing process, new, lower energy levels for electrons are created. When the electrons jump to these lower levels, they emit light. I'll explain fluorescent lights and glow-in-the dark stickers in the Applications section.

More things to do before you read more science stuff

This next activity is one you have to do at night; you'll need a streetlight or a neon sign, so if you don't have those things around the house, you'll have to take a short field trip. First, get your diffraction grating and look through it at a regular light bulb. Take a close look at the rainbows produced. Any gaps in the colors, or is each rainbow continuous?

Now look through the diffraction grating at a streetlight or a neon sign (it will help a lot if these are on at the time). What happens to those nice, continuous rainbows? Any gaps now? In fact, there are lots of gaps. It's as if streetlights and neon signs don't produce all the colors of the rainbow.

Still have the rope or latex tubing around? Good. Tie one end to a fixed object as you did in Chapter 2. Move the free end up and down, slowly at first

---

[1] There are lots of ways we know these things aren't happening, but I'll have to save those for a different book.

---

[2] See the *Stop Faking It!* book *Energy* for a thorough discussion of what we mean by energy.

and then faster. With a little practice, you can produce the patterns shown in Figure 7.3. These are called **standing waves.**

Take note of how fast you move your hand up and down to get the various patterns. When you move your hand up and down faster, we can say that you are increasing the *frequency* at which your hand moves. Now shorten the amount of rope you're using and try for the same patterns. Do they occur at the same frequencies as before?

Figure 7.3

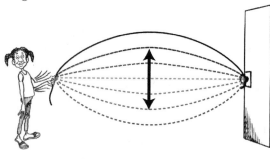

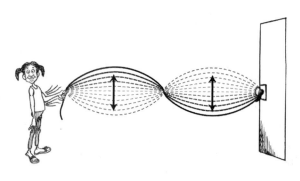

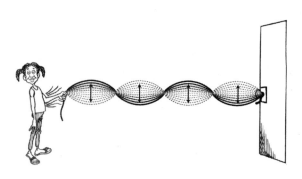

More science stuff

Let's start with the rope. Evidently, the rope has certain frequencies it "likes." When you hit one of those frequencies, you get the neat standing wave patterns. The frequencies at which those patterns occur are known as **resonances.** When you shorten the rope, you get different resonances.[3]

Atoms are a lot like ropes. There are only certain frequencies of light that a given atom will emit, and only certain frequencies of light that an atom will absorb (scientists refer to these as *discrete frequencies*). This is because the allowed energy levels (ledges on the cliff) in an atom are like a fingerprint of the atom. All hydrogen atoms have the same set of energy levels, and all carbon atoms have the same set of energy levels. If there are only certain allowed energy levels in an atom, then there are only certain *differences* in energy between two levels. And here's where **photons** come into the picture. It turns out that

[3] Actually, the tightness of the rope, the thickness of the rope, and what the rope is made of, all affect which frequencies result in standing waves. We're just trying to keep it simple here, though.

you can view light, not as a bunch of waves with a particular frequency, but as a bunch of particles with a particular energy. The picture of light emission then becomes electrons jumping from one energy level to another and emitting a photon as they do that. The energy of that emitted photon is *exactly equal* to the difference in energy between the two levels involved in the jump. See Figure 7.4.

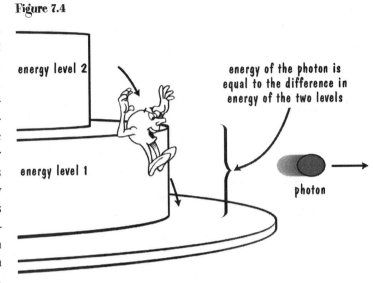

Figure 7.4

energy level 2

energy level 1

energy of the photon is equal to the difference in energy of the two levels

photon

Now, even though we are thinking of the emitted light as a particle (a photon), that light still has a definite frequency in the visible spectrum. In fact, the energy of the photon and the frequency of the emitted light are directly related in the following way:

Energy of photon = (a number)(frequency of emitted light)

The number involved is the same for all photons, and it has a special name—Planck's constant (named after Max Planck, a physicist). Planck's constant is represented by the letter h. Frequency is usually represented by the Greek letter v (pronounced "nu"), so what you'll run into in textbooks is the expression:

$$E = hv$$

We'll stop there before getting too far off track. The important thing to remember is that you can represent light as waves or as particles, and the two models are compatible. For explaining some observations, it's best to think of waves and for others, it's best to think of particles. Okay, one more aside. It turns out that this "wave-particle duality" works not just for light but everything! You can represent protons and neutrons as wave packets or as particles. In fact, you can represent a person as a big bundle of waves. It's not a very useful representation, but you can do it!

Now where were we? Oh yes, individual atoms have only certain allowed energy levels and jumps between energy levels for their electrons. The energy and frequency of any emitted or absorbed light must correspond to the differences in energy between these energy levels. In other words, a given atom can only emit or absorb certain colors of light. You saw that when you looked at a streetlight. Chances are that streetlight contains mercury gas, which glows when you send an electrical current through it. The particular pattern of colors you saw thorough the diffraction grating is mercury's signature. Any time you look at glowing mercury gas through a diffraction grating, you'll see that same pattern.

Okay, so all atoms emit only certain frequencies of light. Why then does an ordinary lightbulb emit a full spectrum of light? Why not just the particular pattern associated with tungsten (what the filament is made of)? The key is that the tungsten filament in a lightbulb is a solid rather than a gas (as is the mercury vapor in a streetlamp). The atoms in a solid are, on average, much closer together than the atoms in a gas. It turns out that when atoms get really close to one another, as in a solid, the energy levels in the atoms get distorted and smeared out. This smearing out of the energy levels results in virtually all of the visible-light energy transitions being possible. Therefore, you get a continuous spectrum. If you excite tungsten *vapor* (a gas), however, then you'll see distinct colors.

To summarize, we now have three different models for what light is—rays, waves, and photons. Each model has its uses, so it's not possible to say that one model is correct and another is incorrect. That's just how it goes with all scientific models, not just those for light. Scientists create pictures and analogies that are correct only to the extent that they explain observations and predict new observations. It's not unusual for a scientific model to explain observations only up to a point. Just because the model breaks down at that point doesn't mean we throw out the model. In the case of light, a ray model doesn't help at all to explain interference, but because it's useful for designing optical instruments, we keep it around. A wave model of light falls apart in certain instances (a classic one is the *photoelectric effect*—look it up in a physics text), but physicists still use a wave model for other things.

The nature of scientific models aside, we haven't covered all of the topics we could with light. As with all the books in this series, the plan is to get your understanding to the point that a) you can teach elementary concepts about light with confidence and b) you are ready to tackle a more traditional textbook if that's what you want to do.

Chapter Summary

- Atoms emit light when their electrons go from a higher energy level to a lower energy level. When atoms absorb light, the electrons go from lower to higher energy levels.

- The energy contained in emitted light is exactly equal to the difference in energy between the two levels involved in an electron transition. The emitted light can be thought of as a series of waves or as a single photon. The energy contained in the photon is equal to $h\nu$, where h is a number known as Planck's constant, and ν is the frequency of the light.

- Different atoms have different sets of characteristic energy levels. Thus, atoms emit discrete frequencies of light that amount to a "fingerprint" of each atom. Such "atomic spectra" are the source of much of what we know about the universe beyond our planet.

Applications

1. What is it that makes laser light so special? Well, when atoms emit light, they do so randomly. There's no overall pattern for when electrons jump levels, so the light is emitted at different times. This means there's no overall phase relationship (whether the light waves are in sync or out of sync) between the waves. In a laser, it's possible to get the electrons of various atoms all at a particular energy level at the same time and keep them there for a while. In this situation, the electrons all have a sort of group mentality. They act as one. When one electron jumps down to a lower energy level, the rest of them go with it all at once (Figure 7.5). It's not unlike lemmings heading over a cliff.

Figure 7.5

When all of the electrons jump at once, the light they emit is all in sync, or in phase. This makes for a very powerful set of light waves, because they all add together constructively. Armed with this explanation, you can understand the words behind the acronym *laser*. The letters stand for "light amplification by stimulated emission of radiation." Makes sense, no?

2. Fluorescent lights contain mercury vapor. When you run an electrical current through the vapor, it excites the mercury atoms. However, in addition to emitting visible light, those atoms emit primarily ultraviolet light. Why then do we see regular light? Because the inside of a fluorescent tube is coated with *phosphors*—molecules that glow when struck by certain frequencies of light or by electrons. The ultraviolet light hits the phosphors, exciting *their* atoms, causing them to emit their own, visible light. We end up with a combination of visible light from the mercury vapor and visible light from the phosphors. By the way, your TV screen also is coated with phosphors. Electron guns (yes, they actually shoot electrons!) hit these phosphors, causing them to glow.

3. I know you're just dying to know how glow-in-the-dark stickers work. Obviously, the source of energy you use to get the sticker electrons into higher energy levels is light itself. You hold the stickers up to a light source, and then they glow for a while. The reason they glow long after the light source is taken away is that the electrons take their sweet time jumping back down to lower energy levels. That's just how the molecules in the stickers are put together. Of course the light emitted by the stickers is never as bright as the original light source because that original input of energy is sent back out over such a long period of time.

4. Astronomers rely heavily on the "light signatures" of atoms (known as atomic spectra) to figure out what's going on in the universe. The particular patterns of light emitted by distant stars can tell us what elements are in the stars, how fast they're moving and in what direction, and whether or not they're rotating. This kind of information is what led to the big bang theory of the creation of the universe.

SCI*LINKS.*
THE WORLD'S A CLICK AWAY

Topic: ultraviolet light

Go to: *www.scilinks.org*

Code: SFL13

Topic: speed of light

Go to: *www.scilinks.org*

Code: SFL14

Glossary

blind spot. The place on the retina of the eye where the optic nerve leaves the eye. The eye cannot detect any image that is formed here, leading to a blind spot in vision. This has nothing to do with the blind spot in your car, where another approaching car is hidden from view by your rearview mirrors.

color addition. The process of combining different-colored light from separate sources to create new colors of light.

color subtraction. The process of using filters or paints to subtract out certain frequencies of light from a single source of white light, producing different colors.

concave lens. A lens that is thinner in the middle than at the edges. See *diverging lens*.

cones. Light receptors that are concentrated in the center of the retina of the eye. Cones detect color well and are most useful in bright light.

converging lens. A lens that bends light inward. Such a lens is thicker in the middle than at the edges. See *convex lens*.

convex lens. A lens that is thicker in the middle than at the edges. See *converging lens*.

critical angle. The angle, measured from the normal to the interface between two mediums, at which light traveling from a more dense to a less dense medium is totally internally reflected.

diffraction. The process by which light traveling through a single slit, or a large number of slits, adds and subtracts, creating a pattern of light and dark fringes. Diffraction is conceptually identical to *interference*.

diffraction grating. A glass or plastic sheet that contains thousands of closely spaced slits. Light traveling through a diffraction grating separates into its component frequencies.

diverging lens. A lens that bends light outward. Such a lens is thinner in the middle than at the edges. See *concave lens*.

electromagnetic spectrum. The range of all possible frequencies of electromagnetic waves, including radio waves, microwaves, visible light, and X rays. The spectrum of visible light is only a tiny fraction of the electromagnetic spectrum.

electromagnetic waves. Waves that consist of changing electric and magnetic fields that propagate even through empty space.

electron. An extremely tiny particle (actually thought of in most applications as a "point object") contained in atoms. When electrons jump from higher to lower energy levels in an atom, they produce light. When electrons absorb light, they jump from lower to higher energy levels.

Fermat's principle. The principle that, in going from one place to another, light rays will always take the path that requires the least amount of time.

fiber optics. Strands of transparent material that use total internal reflection to carry light along the strands, allowing the sending and receiving of information.

focus. The point at which any optical tool (a lens, a reflector, or an antenna) directs incoming parallel light rays.

fovea. The center area of the retina of the eye. The fovea contains primarily cones as receptors.

frequency. The number of wavelengths of light (or sound, or any other kind of wave) that pass a given point per second. Frequency is measured in hertz.

hertz. A unit of frequency that equals 1/second.

index of refraction. A number, related to the density of a medium, that tells how fast light travels in that medium. Comparing the indices of refraction of two mediums will indicate how much light will bend (refract), if at all, when traveling from one medium to the other.

infrared light. Electromagnetic waves that have a slightly lower frequency and slightly longer wavelength than visible light. Infrared light is radiated heat.

interference. The process by which light from two or more slits adds and subtracts, creating a pattern of light and dark fringes. Interference is conceptually identical to diffraction.

laser. A special kind of light in which all the sources of light emit light "in step" or "in phase," leading to a very powerful light beam. Laser stands for *light amplification by stimulated emission of radiation.*

law of reflection. A statement that light incident on a reflective surface and light reflected from that surface make identical angles with the normal line to the surface.

lens. An optical instrument that uses refraction to direct light beams in a desired path.

light. The thing that allows us to see objects. Light can be modeled as rays, electromagnetic waves, or photons. Also something you're supposed to go towards when you die.

medium. A scientific name for a given substance of a given density. Also, the size of drink that costs just a quarter less than a large at the movies, yet still has a price of $3.00.

microwaves. Electromagnetic waves with a lower frequency than infrared waves but a higher frequency than radio waves. Very useful for cooking things.

nanometer. A very small unit of length, equal to 0.000000001 of a meter. Useful for measuring the wavelength of light.

normal line. A line that is perpendicular to a plane surface.

optic nerve. Actually an entire bundle of nerves that take information received by the receptors in the eye and transmit it to the brain.

parabola. A particular curved shape. When used as a reflector, a parabola directs incoming electromagnetic waves to the focus of the parabola, and sends waves emitting from the focus out as parallel rays.

photon. A particle of light that has an energy related to the frequency of the corresponding light wave.

polarized light. Light that has its electric field vibrations oriented in a particular direction, or in a definite pattern of successive directions.

reflection. When light bounces off a surface.

refraction. When light bends in traveling from one medium to another.

retina. The back portion of the eye that contains light receptors.

rods. Light receptors that are concentrated in the outer parts of the retina. Rods are most sensitive in dim light, and do not detect color well.

scattering. The process of light being absorbed, and then reradiated, by atoms and molecules. Rayleigh scattering is the process in which blue light is scattered predominantly in a plane perpendicular to the direction of travel of the light.

Snell's law. A relationship that describes precisely how light will bend, or refract, when traveling from one medium to another. This relationship is written as $n_1 \sin \theta_1 = n_2 \sin \theta_2$, where the index of refraction of medium 1 is n_1 and the index of refraction of medium 2 is n_2. θ_1 is the angle between the incident light ray and the normal line, and θ_2 is the angle between the refracted light ray and the normal line.

total internal reflection. A phenomenon in which light traveling from a more dense to a less dense medium is entirely reflected back into the more dense medium.

transverse waves. Waves that vibrate in a plane perpendicular to the direction of travel of the waves.

ultraviolet light. Light with a slightly higher frequency and slightly shorter wavelength than visible light. "Black lights" emit primarily ultraviolet light.

unpolarized light. Light waves with electric fields that have no pattern of orientation of their direction of vibration.

wavelength. The distance in which a wave repeats its pattern.

X rays. Electromagnetic waves with a frequency greater than visible or ultraviolet light. Useful things for discovering bone fractures.